BRICKBATS AND TUTUS

The amazing story of Julie Felix ~
Britain's first black ballerina

John F Plimmer

This book has been written in memory of
Patrick, Doreen and Lucia Felix and is dedicated
to Julie Felix and her three wonderful daughters,
Amelia, Joanna and Natalie.

Contents

PART ONE

The Early Years

Chapter One

Born to Dance

Dark grey low hanging clouds, honking horns, yellow cabs, loud abusive cabbies and pedestrians chasing from one subway to the next, all hidden beneath a kaleidoscope of bright coloured umbrellas to avoid the heavy downpour. Those were the obstacles which greeted the small coach, as it weaved its way through the deluge, finally stopping outside the rear stage door of one of the city's most famous buildings. They were early, no thanks to the weather and heavy traffic.

Snippets of excited conversation echoed through the adjoining corridors, as the party of dancers made their way to the spacious dressing rooms, anxious and apprehensive, like excited children on a trip to the pantomime. But for one elfin artist, it was only then that the magic really began.

She stood alone on one of the biggest stages in the world, her back as straight as a rod with her head held high, in a phoenix like posture.

Her shiny shoulder length black hair reflected the subdued light sprinkling down from the overheads, resembling moonlight serenading the black Caspian Sea. The house lights in the auditorium were up, but the silence strangely portrayed a void which can only be experienced in an empty theatre. At that moment, her only companions were those of tingling nerve ends, apprehension, hopes and dreams, most of which had followed her throughout her young career. The young lady's large glistening black eyes feasted on the fascinating grandeur of the huge theatre's layers of balconies, stretching from ceiling to floor, supporting red and gold trimmed cushioned seats. The whole scene reminded her of a large multi-tiered birthday cake and she wondered whether all of its four thousand seats would be filled for that night's Gala Performance.

This was not the Sydney Opera House or Piermarini's eighteenth century La Scala in Milan, or the Royal Opera House in Covent Garden. Having been rejected by her country of birth, the Land of the Free had reached out a hand of opportunity, a chance to display her dancing skills to the rest of the world. And now, here she stood, on the boards of one of the most famous buildings on the planet, the Metropolitan Opera House in Lincoln Square, New York. Shortly her dreams were to be accomplished, her frustrations dissolved, her fantasies turned into reality, no matter what the colour of her skin.

"First time at the Met?" the quiet, elderly voice whispered from the wings, in a broad New York accent.

Julie turned to face an old stage hand sporting a mop of grey hair above a friendly face.

She nervously nodded, "I'm one of the lead dancers in tonight's performance."

"That's one hell of an achievement, Miss Felix," he remarked, leaning against some kind of wooden prop, "Just you enjoy the moment. All the way from England eh?"

"I'm trying to, and yes, I'm from London."

"What does your bo' think?"

"I haven't got a boyfriend, I'm a married woman," she answered, wondering what was coming next, "Apart from my husband, my only love has always been for the Ballet since I was a small girl."

The man smiled, his fatherly expression tending to put the girl at ease.

"Well now that figures, but as much as I admire your commitment, that sure is bad news for the rest of the male population. Have a wonderful night and remember if you dance for yourself, you will always please whatever audience turns up to watch you." The old man then turned and disappeared into the darkness of the backstage, beyond where he'd been standing.

She did feel more at ease. The old timer's words had somehow given her confidence. She would dance for herself and let the rest of the world look on in admiration.

It was almost time for the company class, a warm up routine performed daily before each stage performance. But there was still time to take in more of the magnificence of this awesome theatre and her thoughts began to wander back towards her own loved ones.

Julie couldn't avoid a small tear rolling down her cheek, remembering her parents and sister, living so far away in the country of her birth. A country she was determined to return to and earn the plaudits of a British audience, in particular those who had told her she would never make it as a professional ballet dancer.

"...If they are white swans, they all have to be white swans and a black one would just mess up the line," Dame Beryl Gray had once commented, referring to what Julie thought was an opportunity to join a British professional ballet company. But tonight's show in New York, in front of all of those people, would be different.

After the warm up exercises, the time for mental rehearsals soon came to an end. The house lights dimmed and the orchestra struck up. Nerves reached a new crescendo. The stage wings became busy and the theatre filled with wonderful music. Finally, the curtain was raised and the Gala Performance began its mesmerising enthrallment of the audience, with phantoms gliding across the stage, dressed in fleeting and transparent brightly coloured costumes.

Julie stood quietly in the wings, feeling the heat from the overhead lights, staring out at the majestic and graceful adventures dominating the stage; waiting impatiently for her own entrance. It was then she felt a large presence standing beside her. A slight waft of aftershave reached her nose and her eyes glanced up to meet those of the greatest tenor of our time.

There he stood, just inches away, the man she had truly admired and loved throughout her childhood years and still yearned to hear his magnificent voice. Consciously she brushed a bare arm against his jacket sleeve, feeling the thrill. Her nose twitched and her nerve endings went airborne. He was so wide, so big, so sweaty, but all was well. The girl from Ealing, London, had actually physically touched the great man. The master bowed his head and looked down, gently smiling at the girl, showing the whitest teeth she had ever laid eyes on.

"I'm Julie Felix," she announced in a quiet unassuming voice.

"Pleased to meet you, Julie. I am Luciano Pavarotti ..."

1956 was the year when President Nasser of Egypt declared the Suez Canal nationalised by his country, resulting in minor hostilities with the French, British and other interested parties. The Soviet Red Army invaded Hungary and brutally suppressed its people. The first Eurovision song contest was held in Switzerland and the UK charts were dominated by Johnny Ray, Ronnie Hilton and Doris Day. It was also the year Julie Felix was born in the Hammersmith Hospital, West London. As the snow fell and the temperature outside hit below freezing, Doreen and Patrick Felix celebrated the birth of their second daughter, their first, Lucia, had been born eleven months earlier.

Within a few weeks of their younger daughter's entrance into the world, the family moved to Ealing, West London, where they were to live until the mid-eighties. From her earliest days, the frail girl from mixed-race parents was bashful, distrusting and coy. As a three year old, she refused to smile for a professional family photographer, summoned to the home of Patrick Felix to obtain pictures for the family album.

Julie went to Fielding Infants and Junior school before attending the Northfields Senior school in Ealing. As a mere seven year old, her first introduction to dance was encouraged by a young teacher by the name of Miss Bray who had recognised something special in the young black girl. As Julie's natural dancing talent became more prominent, she was encouraged further when told she had an unusual gift which meant she could go far. For the first time in her young life, Jules, as she was called by her father, felt freedom of expression through her performances.

When skipping and twirling around a spacious floor, her mind filled with adventurous peaceful space, believing she was a graceful dove flying high in a cloudless sky; flying low across green meadows surrounded only by Mother Nature. Moving with ease and at one with all the magic the rest of the world could muster. Her natural ability dazzled those who watched and witnessed the kind of grace most other kids didn't possess. As young as she was, Julie would often be given dance themes by her teacher and asked to improvise and interpret. Dance was indeed her salvation.

'There was a star danced, and under that was I born'. William Shakespeare.

Away from the lessons, she would return to her world of shyness and reticence. A fearful world where human intrusion brought discomfort and greater inhibition. She found herself isolated from other children through no fault of her own, except for the colour of her skin. Her mother supported her with only the kind of love a mother can give, but her father, a man less tolerant with minor mishaps, regularly beat her with strap or fist. Patrick was an honest, hard-working West Indian man from Saint Lucia, a foreman maintenance engineer at the Hoover factory, but he was also a man with a temper. His relationship with his younger daughter wasn't helped much by the fact he made no secret of his preferred love for his first born, Lucia, named after her father's birth place. Sadly, that relationship was to dramatically change when both daughters grew older.

As with all schools, the playground provided a meeting place for children's stories to be shared and friendships to develop. Other girls would promise to visit Julie's home to play after school, laughing at the little black girl, but never fulfilling their promise. It wasn't uncommon for the excited child to run home and patiently wait, peering through the curtains of the front room window, for her friends to arrive. It was a regular event for Julie to still be sitting there as dusk came, sobbing and confused as to the reason why she had been so cruelly snubbed. She wasn't much older than when she had been given her first dancing lesson, when she realised the colour of her skin was different to other girls in the school and she prayed each night to be white like the rest of them. She often tried to straighten her beautiful black hair to make it look like the others, but never really succeeded.

Each morning she would awaken, only to find she was still black and that God had not answered her prayers. She would then cry some more, until her tears would turn to bitterness in realisation that she was no different from those other girls and perhaps even better than them. After all, she had a God-given gift. She had been born to dance and that's exactly what this little girl was so hell bent on doing, from that tender age onwards.

'To be born to dance is true. It's a condition. It's in the cells; the tissues and in the essence of who you are. Selfishness then becomes selflessness.' Julie Felix

Chapter Two

Early Success

The long icy cold spell that dominated the winter and spring months of 1963 broke records for being the most prolonged cold spell in living memory. Pipes burst, roof tiles cracked, rail tracks became unsafe for use, the most vulnerable people perished and radiators in lorries transporting supplies to retailers, split wide open. The country for many months remained virtually immobilised.

It was on one of those bitterly cold days, when icicles dominated eaves and human faces remained hidden behind curtains and thick woolly scarves, that Doreen Felix and her daughter Julie decided it was time to feed the local ducks. Both mum and her youngest offspring huddled together, heading for the nearby frozen pond, leaning against the icy wind with the girl grasping their offerings, a bag full of stale bread. It was food for survival from starvation, that's if you were a duck.

The excited Julie began to throw the welcome feast to her feathered friends, which wasted no time in quickly making a beeline towards their saviour. It was when the girl noticed one Mallard in particular, sitting motionless on the ice towards the middle of the pond, that she decided to launch a javelin throw towards the seemingly disinterested duck. Stretching her arm back as far as it would go, she hurled the largest piece of bread taken from the bag, towards the waiting recipient. Unfortunately the momentum of her frail body continued with the missile and her mother looked on as Julie also went flying across the ice, to land near the stranded Mallard.

There were screams as the girl broke through the ice and found herself up to her neck in freezing Arctic water. The cold was immense, so much so, she couldn't control her trembling face. Luckily, the water wasn't deep enough to cover her and she fought with all her strength to break through the ice until she made it back to mum's safe outstretched arms, shivering and blue.

"If you wasn't so thin and ate all of your dinners, that would never have happened," Julie's mother frantically shouted at her daughter. But there wasn't much time to say anything else, Julie was quickly freezing to death and had to be returned home as soon as humanly possible. Both mother and daughter raced back towards where they lived, with cold water squelching in small boots and Julie's heavy winter's coat, much heavier.

Of course they made it before Mrs. Felix's daughter turned into a small iceberg, but there were consequences and the frail youngster became very ill for weeks after that episode. Have no fear, it was the first and last time she felt any desire to get more personal with the local ducks.

The family home was a terraced house with a narrow, lengthy alleyway, which gave access to the back gardens in which Julie would often be seen playing. But the little girl's favourite hideaway place was nearby Lamas Park, where she could play on swings and roundabouts, in similar fashion to any other child. But Julie was different from any other child. Swinging high towards the sky had the same effect as when she was dancing; she felt a sensation of freedom and peace, as her frail body lifted higher and higher. If only she had wings to launch herself upwards into the sky, to join those birds of free rein and stay with them, looking down at a world that was so hostile towards her.

Her mother used to worry about her daughter being on the receiving end of some untimely accident and often voiced concerns about having to cross a busy road to reach the park. She always insisted Julie returned home before tea time and before darkness fell, which being the attentive girl she was, always did so. She loved her mother very much.

The terraced house in which they lived was also different from the others. It was the most colourful in the street, Julie's father deciding to show his pride in his residence by painting it all the colours of the rainbow. In fact, he changed the colour of his front door as an annual event, with a burning desire to make the building stand out from any other in their row. That was the vast extent of his domestic pride. It also sent out a message to everyone in the neighbourhood that this was his house and he'd paint his door any colour he bloody well chose. He certainly achieved that and one thing was certain, every passerby knew the house was lived in by a West Indian gentleman.

The Felixes lived just a ten minute walk from Julie's school, but that wasn't always plain sailing for the youngest member. In those days London fogs were notorious and when such a thick fall of grey and yellow grime-filled smog hit the neighbourhood, it was difficult to see more than a yard or two in front. Julie would often walk to school alone, unlike other girls who would have friends accompanying them, but of course they were all white. When the fog came down, she could only find her way by following one building line after another, in fear of her life and in the hope that she would make the school gates without being suddenly swooped off her feet by some gigantic eagle, or other bird of prey. Away from home she often felt alone and unwanted and the smell of sulphur that used to accompany the fogs, plus the fear she felt, was to remain in her memory for the rest of her life.

The future professional ballet dancer already attended at St Paul's Church, Ealing, and it was in that same year, as the temperatures persisted to freeze the nation, Julie joined Joyce Butler's School of

Dance. Classes were held in the church hall and budding pupils would be taught ballet, tap and other forms of entertaining dance. Unfortunately and disappointingly for Julie, little teaching was done on specialised subjects. It was all a matter of what each child appeared to be good at, or rather, what Joyce Butler thought each child was better at. The seven year old was still a small dove in need of freedom and open skies, which she could fill with amazing rhythm and grace. Her tutor, Joyce Butler, tended to focus more on summer season movements and pantomime, which seemed to be more suitable for the rest of the young class.

Eventually, Julie was told quite candidly that she would never make it as a ballet dancer. Why was that? Was it because she was too small, which would have been strange considering she was taller than most of the other kids, or was it because she was black and people needed time to get to know her better, perhaps to ease their conscience and lose their immoral bias towards her? Once again an obstacle had suddenly appeared in her young life, one which had to be confronted and surmounted. When she asked the reason why she would be a failure, she was told she was too skinny. Julie was also aware the only other girl in the class who was the recipient of a similar accusation that ballet would never be her forte, just happened to also be black. Nevertheless, Julie continued attending lessons for the following two years.

She became a Brownie at the same church, then a Girl Guide, her mother encouraging her to mix more with other children, but avoidance from other children continued and the colour of her skin remained a constant talking point amongst others. At night her pillow was still saturated with her tears.

She had difficulty in recalling that period of her young life with any pleasure and apart from the infantile racism she had to endure, there were other obstacles that made her existence even more problematic. An eating disorder plagued her throughout those early years, only later to be diagnosed as a food allergy to wheat and one or two other of nature's provisions thrown down her throat. Ignorant of that fact, teachers, in particular her Senior School Headmistress Miss Hubbard, demanded the frail black girl consumed all that was put on her school dinner plate, but Julie was defiant and used to spit out most of her food into a handkerchief for later disposal.

The initial enthusiasm Julie had for the dancing lessons began to dwindle under the constant pressure of being isolated by the other children and some of the teachers. Although she was never told the reasons why she was made to feel so alone, and ignored when questioning anything she felt was important, the colour of her skin had to be a part of the equation. A sad and lonely period of her life followed and she began to feel trapped inside herself. Various emotions became bottled up inside the girl, a mixture of frustration, confusion, inhibition and many others were responsible for a sense of unhappiness and her failure to release those feelings, added to their increasing influence.

Finally, she spoke with her mother and asked to return to dancing.

"Julie, if that's what you want to do, then do it," her mother advised, "We will support you financially and with my blessing. It doesn't matter a hoot what other children think."

So, as an eleven year old, Julie returned to the Joyce Butler's School of Dance, but this time with vengeance in her heart and a determination to succeed, no matter what others thought about her shape and size. The fact that her mother was married to a black man would no longer torment her; her ears would remain closed to the distasteful puns and jibes thrown at her by others of her same age. She danced and danced, working hard on the highly polished, uneven floorboards inside the church hall; never missing an opportunity to rise back into those open blue skies, like a bird of freedom. It was Julie's way of releasing those built up emotions fuelled by her constant fear of being rejected because of the colour of her skin, similar to steam hissing through an open valve, re-energising those ambitions which had never actually left her.

She took ballet exams and entered competitions run weekly across the London Region, winning more than she lost. She sang solo and demonstrated feather like movements, which added elegance and charm to her performances. Her mind was heading in a different direction, as her earlier frustrations and disappointments were replaced by guile and a strong determination to succeed. Her success helped to evaporate any self-doubts she might have had about her future as a professional dancer and her love for the stage became total.

She would spend hours watching her mother dress up for various amateur operatic performances, sitting in wonderment at the grease paint, large fancy dresses and glittering costume jewellery that turned her mater into an apparition of beauty and joy. The exhilaration of such observations was infectious, so influential on her young mind that nothing said or done would ever again diminish the hunger and passion she was feeling for a life time spent on the boards, pleasing audiences and receiving plaudits she so earnestly craved for.

Tring Park Arts Educational School became known to Julie. First opened in 1939 the school recruited young people who could show they had an outstanding talent for the performing arts and the school boasted amongst its pupils, Dame Julie Andrews and Dame Beryl Bainbridge. At the same time, successful applicants would continue to receive an academic education. Such a stepping stone was an irresistible challenge for the black talented young dancer; a challenge which she accepted with relish, having no hesitation when deciding to apply.

She spoke to her dance instructor Joyce Butler and outlined her plans to gain entrance into Tring Park. At first, Butler was extremely discouraging, telling her not to bother, again begging the question, why was this, when the dance teacher's principle objective was to support and encourage her young pupils. Had the colour of the girl's skin been influential once again? But Julie was well past compliance and her defiance resulted in a phone call requesting an application form. When the necessary paperwork arrived through the post, she excitedly answered the required questions before returning the application together with a photograph of herself. She didn't have to wait long for a reply and shortly afterwards the best news she was hoping for, came back; she had been invited to audition at the school.

The success must have pricked her dance teacher's way of thinking and Julie's enthusiasm finally persuaded Joyce Butler to support her by putting together a dance routine for her young student, to be accompanied by a rendition of Julie Andrews, 'My Favourite Things.' She rehearsed and rehearsed again and then some.

When the great day finally arrived, she travelled to the former Rothschild Mansion in Hertfordshire, accompanied by her mother. Surrounded by a countryside of beauty and within the walls of an amazingly majestic former stately home, the little black girl from Ealing, London, mesmerised her audience by singing and dancing in the only way Julie Felix could, making Doreen Felix the proudest mother in the universe.

She was offered a place at the school, almost immediately, but further disappointment was to dog her ambitions. The fees were extravagant and nigh on impossible for her family to meet over a lengthy period of time. After many tears and confused thoughts, she finally accepted that the latest obstacle to her life-long ambition was a mere blip. But, by then she was becoming stronger, her self-belief was heading beyond self-doubt. She was becoming used to being knocked back, in similar fashion to a puppy taking a daily beating from its master. Her resolve grew and by looking in the mirror she began to see the kind of determination possessed only by the few, those who achieve and those who are first past the winning post.

Chapter Three

An unusual Christmas Treat

The house lights dimmed and the conductor raised his baton, bringing the orchestra into life as the music began to play softly, and the curtain lifted. This was the real beginning for the young twelve year old girl who found it all so exhilarating and experiencing the thrill of her young life. Julie sat in one of the luxurious red and gold trimmed seats with both eyes wide open and her gaping mouth catching flies. The whole atmosphere inside the auditorium was filled with so much anticipation she could feel it, live it, almost touch it. A mixture of warm exciting odours, with wafts of expensive perfume being the most dominant, added to the adventure and then she blinked and jumped as the orchestra suddenly and without warning, turned up the sound.

Her mother sat beside her, throwing covert glances across at her daughter's astonished facial expression, seemingly frozen in time, in total concentration and bewilderment, as the theatre filled with the most wonderful and gratifying sound of Jessye Norman's operatic voice. This was undoubtedly the best Christmas present Doreen Felix could have ever given to her little girl with all that hard earned cash, a night at the opera, a night at one of the world's most famous seats of artistic culture at its very best, the Royal Opera House, Covent Garden. All the glamour, beauty and delivery intended to show Julie the standard required to be a great stage professional, where hard work and the kind of dedication that was second to none, was required to reach the top. She had high hopes for her youngest daughter and felt only sadness that her oldest daughter, Lucia, didn't possess or show any interest in the arts. Lucia would take a totally different path, which would end with unhappiness and disaster, not that anyone was aware of that fact, at that particular time.

Of course her husband, Patrick, would never have agreed to spending so much money on just a pair of tickets to watch an opera, so she hadn't told him, this was between herself and Julie. Of course he would eventually find out, probably after they had returned home and their daughter wanted to tell the whole world about the wonders of that night, but he would just moan and groan and throw a couple of dissenting remarks Doreen's way. But that mattered not to the woman who had served as a WAF during the war, driving heavy lorries which transported parachutes. How that life seemed so far away now, remembering how she and her best friend Jesse, used to visit local public houses and chase Scots Guardsmen round the tables to see if any of them were wearing anything beneath their kilts.

She smiled to herself as the first performance came to an end and the audience stood to applaud.

"Mum, this is just fantastic, thank you," Julie said with sincerity.

"I am so glad you are enjoying the performance, now be careful, don't over excite yourself, the night is early yet."

Doreen came from Rainham in Essex and was a member of the Ealing Amateur Operatic Society. She first met Patrick on a bench in Hyde Park and they hit it off instantly. They openly courted each other, ignoring the jibes and nasty remarks thrown at them about a white woman going with a black man. As far as Doreen was concerned she had fallen in love with the most handsome man in the universe. And Patrick Felix was handsome, lean and tall, a man who loved all that there was about American culture, although he never actually visited the United States, even during the years Julie was performing there. Being a big fan of Humphrey Bogart, he was a smart dresser, his attire frequently resembling the 1940's wide bottom trouser suits, with spats covering brightly polished shoes.

Although a harsh man when it came to disciplining his daughter, Julie, he was also a man who lived by certain principles and a grafter who rarely missed a day as foreman at the Hoover Building on Western Avenue, Perivale, West London. He was the provider and central figure of his family, rarely interfering with domestic situations, but making his thoughts known quite vociferously when he thought it necessary. He also kept the daily problems he had to face from the racist taunts regularly thrown his way like confetti from white people who Patrick could only regard as ignorant and misinformed, well outside the family home.

It came as quite a shock when one late afternoon in 1965 he returned home early from work, covered in blood. His wife gasped and his two daughters ran to help him stagger those last few steps to his front door, confused and impatiently waiting for their father's story to unfold.

It transpired that, in his position as foreman at the Hoover Factory, Patrick had become involved in an argument with a fellow worker, some guy who had obviously refused to accept defeat in whatever verbal conflict had taken place. So, in seeking violent revenge in return for the humiliation suffered, the same man waited outside the factory gates for Mr. Felix to leave.

As soon as Patrick had cleared the company's building he was attacked with a vicious heavy hook attached to the end of a metal chain. The hook had been driven in deep across the foreman's shoulders and neck and other workmates had run to assist their foreman, helping him back inside the factory, where he was given First Aid before making his way home.

It was common practice in those days not to inform the Police and the same applied in Patrick's case. After all, he later told his wife and daughters, the attack took place outside the factory premises so what was the point in making a mountain out of a mole hill. Abiding by their father's wishes, nothing more was ever discussed about the incident and Patrick returned to work the following day as if nothing had happened.

Another Act ended and the audience again stood to applaud, including Julie and her mother. They were seated right up in the 'Gods' as they were the cheapest tickets and the only ones that Doreen could afford. She loved to see Julie looking so thrilled and enthusiastic, obviously being carried away on some magic carpet with everything that was going on around her.

As they returned to their seats, she continued to watch the next Act, still thinking back to those earlier days before she and Patrick were married. Her father wasn't that much dissimilar to how her future husband behaved, another man with high principles and a disciplined approach to just about everything which crossed his path. Doreen remembered when Patrick met her father and asked for her hand in marriage. Captain Kirk and the whole crew of the Starship Enterprise might just as well have been beamed down on to the carpet of her parents' front room, by the look of shock on the old man's grey bearded face. When the request was made, her father began to spin, not knowing whether to look for his pipe under an armchair or up a chimney.

"Are you alright, sir?" Patrick asked, wondering whether some kind of virus had struck the old man down, turning him into a revolving door. When the door finally stopped, those present waited in anticipation, Doreen hoping, praying that the next few words spoken would be, 'Congratulations my good man, you have my blessings and hopes for a bright and happy future.' But all of that went out of the window, after the old man finally picked up his pipe from the hearth and with his head bowed to show off his vague middle parting, mumbled something under his breath.

"I'm sorry, sir, I didn't quite catch that," Patrick explained.

Doreen's elderly father lifted his head as if a spring had just broken in his neck and said in a louder voice, "I wasn't bloody well talking to you."

He then turned his eyes towards his daughter and declared, "If you get married to a black man, we will disown you, you can be sure of that."

Well, so much for, let's all piss in the same pot people and move forward as one. Patrick must have wished for Martin Luther King to have been present to give the old goat one of his rousing sermons, but alas, knowing the stubbornness of the kind of man his future father in law was, he decided to just leave it at that.

So it came to pass, the loving couple did get married without Doreen's father's blessing and while they were getting wed in a local church, the old man remained at home practicing his revolving door routine, with Doreen's best friend Jesse, having to give her away. Initially the newlyweds lived in a small flat in Hammersmith before moving to Ealing just after Julie was born.

Jessye Norman came to the end of her final performance and bowed as the uproar from the audience was deafening. Doreen Felix's eyes were moist and she also stood up, watching her daughter jump up and down, clapping hard and even mimicking others in the audience by shouting, "Bravo, bravo."

"So what did you think of it all, Julie, have you enjoyed yourself?" her mother asked, as they left the theatre to catch a bus home, already knowing the answer.

"Oh Mum," the girl replied, "I have never been so happy, thank you for a wonderful Christmas present."

So, Mum was also pleased, she had hoped Julie would have been ecstatic seeing her first professional operatic performance and the fact she was, gave Doreen the best Christmas present she could have wished for. Then the twelve year old Julie posed a question to her mother.

"Do you think I could ever be an opera singer, Mum, like that beautiful black lady we've just seen?"

"No, Julie, your destiny lies down another path. Opera and Ballet both have similar disciplines, but your natural gift for dancing is the path you must take. To reach the end of that path will require a lot of hard work, probably in your case, harder work than most people."

"Because I'm black, Mum?"

Doreen stopped and looked down at her girl before answering, "No, Julie, because in this world of ours there are a lot of very ignorant and biased people, my love, who will do their utmost to stand in your way."

Chapter Four

Musical Theatre

Julie's enthusiasm for The Ballet didn't dwindle after leaving school and the long hours and hard work continued at Joyce Butler's School of Dance, with some encouragement from her mother. She was no longer isolated, she had found new friends; courage, commitment and self-motivation were always there to offer a hand of inspiration.

One of her final school day successes was to obtain a coveted Pitman's qualification in touch typing and she intended to put that to good use. Her love for the ballet the ballet was still as strong as ever and if she could spend every hour of every day, practicing, that would have been her preference, but she had to earn money for the household, which meant attending dance lessons whenever she could, but putting paid work at the top of her agenda. Julie followed in her father's footsteps, obtaining employment as a touch typist at the Hoover Company, but all was not as it first seemed.

The girl's first day was spent hidden away in a small, high walled and windowless cubicle, with only one typewriter and a stock pile of folders containing hand written documents, awaiting their transformation into print. The difficulty she experienced from the very first, was the frustrating and soul-destroying way in which one completed folder of work was immediately replaced with another, guaranteeing there would never be an end in sight to the mountain of paperwork that awaited her attention. Every time the little man with the bald head and spectacles that resembled the bottoms of milk bottles, stepped inside her small retreat from the rest of humanity, she asked if the continuous production of paperwork was ever shut down. Unfortunately for Julie, the paper freak had no sense of humour and would just turn and leave without saying a word, after topping up the pile of folders to be typed, of course.

It was all a complete waste of time, as far as she was concerned and fair enough, the only other experience she had during that stay at the Hoover factory was tired fingers. Fortunately for youngsters in those days, jobs were so frequently advertised there was no shortage of work for those who wanted it. So, when she left at the end of that first day, Julie didn't return.

Surprisingly, her next position in the world of the paid workers, found her working for the Zambian High Commission, one of her daily tasks being to take confidential papers from the Commission's main office to another location in Oxford Street. Feeling that she had become part of some kind of James Bond network, she was thrilled and excited when chauffeur driven across London with documents she had previously been made to swear she would never rest her eyes on. God knows what conspiracies they contained.

What 'M' wasn't aware of was that Julie used to unofficially disappear most afternoons and mosey across the City to the Pineapple Dance Studio in Covent Garden, where she took on further ballet lessons in addition to those ongoing at Joyce Butler's School of Dance in the church hall. It was a delight to be able to practice for once, on floorboards that didn't resemble uneven piano keys.

Her settled lifestyle pattern continued for some time. Remaining at the Zambian High Commission each morning to complete whatever work she was given, then off to Oxford Street in the chauffeur driven car, secret documents to hand and guarded with her life, then off to her ballet lessons. What more could a young girl require? But, time went by without further encouragement from any source except those old reliable friends, courage, commitment and self-motivation. The hard work she was putting in daily, yielded nothing in return. More rejections were thrown at her from various people in the dancing profession who didn't hold back their punches when informing Julie, 'Sorry darling, you just don't have the ability."

Verbal argumentative exchanges became a common occurrence and a 'Oh no she hasn't, Oh yes she has,' persuasion began to dominate her thoughts. An internal jousting contest began to formulate, resulting in confusion, not helped by a distinct lack of direction, or help in identifying the right path down which she should go. She began to feel like the spinning rotary arm of a helicopter until she finally decided to rid her mind of all of the bewilderment slowly disorienting her thought patterns and targeted the musical theatre, with, of course, encouragement from Joyce Butler, who specialised in that particular dance version. Sadly, the girl's love for Classical Ballet had to be put on the back burner, although she had no intention of hanging up her pointe shoes for good.

So, her life-style and future plans changed dramatically. After all, perhaps all those invisible faces, teachers and other kids at school who had treated her so subordinately because she was black, perhaps they had been right when they laughed at the idea of a black person entering the world of Classical Ballet. It was the first and only time a dent appeared in her armour and she eventually auditioned for her first pantomime, *Mother Goose* at the Theatre Royal in Bath, rubbing shoulders with hundreds of other potential professional dancers.

She found the whole episode demeaning, having to stand on a stage with a number stuck to her back, performing a set routine in front of a panel of stone-faced producers, whose communicative skills were limited to just a couple of words, "Next please." She stood by and watched her young competitors, as they ran for cover in the stage wings, tears streaming down their innocent faces. Their words were basically the same, "What are they looking for, for Christ's sake? I have just danced my heart out and they didn't like me."

"Next please."

Then an unknown voice sounded from somewhere behind Julie and quietly said, "Don't give up, girl, you can do this." So she did. She danced for her mother, father and sister and above all, for herself, her very soul. She danced as though her life depended upon it, moving and gliding through the air like some light weight nymph in celebratory mood, feeling the freedom, the excitement, the excellence of the dance. She gave it everything, leaning on all those years of hard work and initiative, hearing class instructors' voices penetrating her mind, amplifying the requirements of what she was portraying.

At the end, she found herself totally exhausted, never having before put so much physical and mental energy into one dance routine. She waited in the wings on all fours, praying she had done enough to impress that battlement of indifferent expressions that had watched from the third row back.

Eventually, the results were made known to the tears and expressions of false confidence. The numbers were called out as if the whole event had now turned into a game of Tombola, but Julie's number wasn't called. It was time for her to go home, back to the drawing board, back to the emptiness and frustration that had been dogging her, causing her to temporarily forget about her one true love, Classical Ballet.

Then the surprise came. A small man with grey hair and a smiling face spoke quietly to her, telling her to go to the office and collect the necessary paperwork. She recognised the man's voice as being the same that had earlier told her not to give up. She had done it. Julie had finally landed her first Equity paying job. Julie was now a professional dancer and although it wasn't to be a role in a Ballet, she felt exhilarated by the success of having achieved all day dancing as an earner. She couldn't wait to tell her parents and share her success with her dance instructor, Joyce Butler, who had never hidden her disbelief that a black dancer would ever break into the professional arena. So, it was farewell to the Zambian High Commission and hello to the City of Bath.

For the first time in her young life, Julie left home and was away for three months, rehearsing with the rest of the cast for *Mother Goose*, but more problems weren't far away. The wardrobe mistress of the theatre made it quite clear, she wasn't at all happy with Julie's slim, ballet-like body and told her that her bosom was way too small for the kind of dancing she was undertaking. The real reason for the lady's concerns was that she had to alter all of the costumes Julie was required to wear during her performances.

So, riding crop and fishnet tights were kept in safe storage as she danced, virtually non-stop throughout that panto season, six days a week, eight shows a week. And yet, although the work involved kept her in peak condition, something was missing. Julie's individual performances were way above the standard required and that fact was reiterated by other members of the cast, as well as the production team. One fellow member once told her, "Lady, you should think about training up for The Ballet!" That was indeed a bitter pill to swallow.

As the weeks passed by and the performances became more intense, Julie's feeling of emptiness increased. She was becoming a serious victim of wanting, desiring something not within her reach; the youngster felt she was unable to feel the kind of satisfaction she needed to feel. Something was seriously wrong and she knew deep down, it was the absence of harsh discipline experienced in Classical Ballet. The stimulating sensation of freedom wasn't there. This was not for Julie and she knew then that the yearning she was feeling for The Ballet would never agree to leave her. Courage, commitment and self-motivation were joining forces and messing about with her head. The confusion she had previously experienced was returning with a vengeance.

Following the season's end, she returned home and began searching for something that would propel her to a higher level. Damn the doubters, damn those who had little time for a black ballet dancer and damn the bloody snobbery that was preventing her from fulfilling her real, true vocation. There had to be something out there, something that would satisfy her growing hunger and desperation. To fall at the first hurdle didn't necessarily mean you lost the race.

Julie's experience of musical theatre had not been wasted. She now knew many of the ups and downs of being a professional dancer. However, she also knew her own destiny and her love for The Ballet had been rekindled, as was her commitment to succeed by hook or by crook. Persistence was the key, a trait in which Julie abounded. It was time for a reality check, time to not just knock on doors but to hammer them down. Like a boxing world title challenger about to enter the ring, she spent time mentally adjusting, tuning those nodules of doubt into non-existence, nurturing and strengthening her resolve. The time had come to ignore the negative comments coming from those who she would only regard as adversaries. A new campaign was on the horizon and this time she would be merciless in achieving her ambition and aims. She would open that elusive door to that world which had previously denied her. But what she needed before entering the affray once again was a strategy, one which would guide her along the right path, beginning with the most renowned school of dance where she would achieve success.

Applying for an audition for the Royal Ballet School would be futile, because she knew that no black dancer had ever been accepted before into what was regarded as the headquarters of Classical Ballet, but she could at least enquire. Just one phone call to the school and talking with one of the staff there, confirmed her fears when she was told that she virtually had no chance of being accepted because of the colour of her skin. She was also told she was too young in any case, which confused Julie before realising that suggestion was utter tripe, the real reason for rejection being that she was black. So, she wasn't prepared to waste time attempting the impossible and turned her attention in another direction, targeting the Rambert Ballet School with all its credibility and reputation for turning out students of the highest quality.

The initial process wasn't easy. Firstly she had to write off for an application form, then return that document to Rambert together with photographs of herself in various ballet poses. If the School considered her application good enough, then an audition followed.

Julie didn't have to wait long after returning the necessary documents and an invitation for an audition quickly landed on the floor of her parents' hallway. Of course she was pleased with the result of her plan thus far, but some of those earlier doubts were still there, hiding like black faceless carrion crows in the depths of her mind, armed with only bad news. She became convinced the photographs of the ballet poses she had sent to Rambert with her application form, had been responsible for getting her the audition, which they had. But Julie believed the reason they had made their mark was only because, in the colourless snaps, she had resembled a white girl. As hard as she might try, she could not expel those old doubts that constantly attacked her self-belief. She couldn't steer her beliefs away from what she had been told so many times in the past, that black dancers could never be acceptable in The Ballet. She also knew that such detrimental thoughts could be turned around and the very thought of being at a disadvantage over other white students of the Dance, could be her knight in shining armour. The drive she needed to propel her to greater things and evidence that the doubters were nothing short of bloody mindlessness.

Chapter Five

From Elation to Despair

This was to be the biggest step forward in Julie Felix's young life, provided she got through the audition for entrance into the Rambert School. She and hundreds of other applicants were met by the founder's daughter, Miss Angela Ellis, and the young girl from Ealing was impressed by the lady principal's appearance. She was an ornate woman, with the largest pair of earrings Julie had ever seen and the kind of cultured voice that the young girl thought could only be heard on television or radio. But above all, Dame Marie Rambert's daughter addressed all the young hopefuls assembled, with a calming and reassuring soft voice. There was no time for nervous twitches or anxiety or panic attacks. This was the one opportunity Julie was determined to grasp with both hands.

The auditions began and the potential dancers were asked to perform the most gruelling tasks, certainly the most difficult Doreen Felix's daughter had ever encountered. But, on this occasion, the final results were not made known and the applicants were asked to return to their homes where they would eventually be notified as to their success or failure. Although Julie believed she had done enough during her audition, how could she be sure and what would she do next if her fate was decided in the negative?

It was the most agonising period in her young life, waiting to hear whether the audacity of her first real move into Classical Ballet had paid off. Of course, that old doubt banged away in her mind. Had she succeeded as a result of her polished performance at Rambert, or was she once again, to be cast aside because of the colour of her black skin? She truly believed though, that this time she had been judged on her performance by Miss Ellis and her staff members. Only time would tell.

A week later, on the Saturday morning following her audition, Julie was getting ready to skip off for a lesson with Joyce Butler, when the post arrived. Her mother called for her to come downstairs, having picked up the small white envelope addressed from the Rambert Ballet School. Excitement filled the air and for a short period both mother and daughter looked at each other in anticipation, not knowing whether to open the envelope and read its contents, or cast it to one side and pretend it had never arrived.

Julie's mother was concerned, not knowing what kind of effect another devastating rejection would have on her daughter's mental stability. Julie was concerned that she might have fallen at the first hurdle of her new reborn dedication and ambition, following that short excursion into musical theatre.

Still, they continued to stare at each other, until finally the silence between them was filled with her mother's whispering words.

"Julie, love, it's a small white envelope. It may be bad news."

"Yes," her daughter replied softly, "But yet again, a small white envelope might mean I've been accepted, Mum."

Why the hell didn't they just open the damned envelope and put themselves out of the miserable environment their inquisitiveness was creating?

"Shall I open it?" her mother asked.

Julie nodded, nervously, as if that small white object was in reality, a hand grenade and by pulling out the pin, all around them would instantly disappear.

She stood on shaky legs and watched as her mother slowly broke the seal and carefully removed the letter from its pouch. Then her eyes gave it away, filling with pools of tears and her mouth opening into a wide gap, as she gasped for more air.

Finally, the words were spoken that Julie would remember for the rest of her life. They were simple words, nothing grand or taken from any classical piece of poetry, "You're in love, you're in."

The small piece of paper confirming Julie's entrance dropped to the floor as they both embraced, stepped back, cried and then embraced again. At last, at long last, her best friends, courage, commitment and self-motivation had pulled her through. The breakthrough had come and that young girl suddenly knew, her life would never ever be the same again. Neither would Doreen Felix's. Angela Ellis had sent proof of her belief in Julie's talent and not in the colour of her skin. The faith Dame Marie Rambert's daughter had shown, would be repaid by the bucketful.

They say that fate moves in mysterious ways. That was certainly the case as far as Julie Felix was concerned. It took just a few hours to turn the girl's elation into one of unexpected despair. She wanted to tell the world of her success and did so, explaining to everybody she met about her life changing achievement. As the rain came down in torrents, the coatless girl with the black frizzy hair sang and danced her way around the streets of Ealing. People in the corner shop listened intently and nodded their appreciation of Julie's good fortune. Road sweeps were met with excited chatter; people who she didn't know by name, were stopped on the street and given an informative explanation as to why everywhere she went she skipped. Even the local copper on the beat was made to park his bicycle while his ears were filled with the same lines of excited jabber. Julie's high spirited joy spread like wild fire throughout the neighbourhood. Then she returned home, dripping wet from nose and chin, not that she noticed.

Her mother stood in the doorway, the almost apologetic expression of sadness obvious. "It's not good news, love," she whispered, "It's the fees for Rambert. We just cannot afford to pay for them. They are much too high for us."

It was indeed bad news, after all Julie had been through, the worst kind of news she could have been given. It was as though an explosive charge made up of shrapnel coated in frustration, anger and bewilderment had gone off inside her head. For most young girl's such a disclosure of wreckage would have been the end, but not for this particular girl. This particular lady had been through too much. Her resolve had been tested to the limit on so many occasions before and in similar fashion to that boxing world title challenger who hit the canvas in the first round, she was determined to get back on her feet and throw a few punches of her own.

Defeat was not on the table, neither was a soft surrender, no matter how big the obstacle. Those three major allies, courage, commitment and self-motivation were once again summoned to the surface and there was no way on Earth she was going to let this opportunity get washed down the sink. She had done her bit, all that had been required to propel her future forward, to continue her love affair with what she believed in. Yes, she had done her bit. There was no way she was now going to fall yet again at the final hurdle. It was back to the grindstone, the planning, scheming, hoping, praying and anything else that would destroy the obstacle blocking her way, money.

In desperation, Julie explored all possible avenues, which might facilitate funding. There was nothing on the horizon, until she heard about the Inner London Education Authority affording grants to the very talented, albeit in limited supply. Well, she was very talented and doubted there was any other living creature qualified for such a grant, more than she. There certainly wasn't any other living creature with as much determination as she had, so further enquiries followed and eventually the application forms arrived, asking personal questions, including details of her parents' finances.

At first her father disagreed with what she was doing, believing her daughter was seeking nothing more than charity. So what? If it meant a future in the world for which she craved so much. Her mother remained positive and helped out where she could. Another audition followed, just to confirm that this particular black girl had the required level of talent necessary for money to be spent on her. In fact, a whole lot of money, which would involve payments for a three year Classical Ballet course, not to mention pointe shoes, other equipment and clothing. Fortunately, living in London with the Dance School situated in the same region of the country, Nottinghill Gate, board and lodgings wouldn't be a problem. Julie would be staying at mum and dad's for the duration.

The hardened determination which was driving Julie on, finally paid off. The grant was facilitated, which meant that seventy five percent of all expenses would be met by the ILEA and her parents would have to find the remainder, which was a better deal than the one they faced before their daughter had applied. Even Patrick managed a wry smile as he put yet another coat of paint on that fluorescent front door. Now, once again the coast was clear and her fate determined. Now, she could prove all the doubters that she, a black girl from Ealing, could become the best ballet dancer, her skills and character would allow.

Ballet Rambert, as it was known from 1935 to 1987 was first formed by Marie Rambert, a Polish lady born to a Russian mother and Polish-Jewish father in Warsaw in 1888. With some help from her husband, Ashley Dukes, an English playwright, critic and theatre manager, she first opened the Ballet Club in 1930 using her husband's Mercury Theatre in Notting Hill Gate, for a group of talented artists who used to meet up for regular Sunday performances. Rambert's commitment to The Ballet helped to create and strengthen a ballet community in Britain and she received many plaudits for her life-long work, together with Dame Ninette de Valois, who was the founder of what became The Royal Ballet.

Young Julie was ready to be accepted into such exultant company. She would work like no other had. She would face every task put before her with pride and belief. She would succeed where others had failed. After all, she now knew she had something special. Something that a person is born with and Julie Felix had been born to dance.

Part Two

The Rambert Years

Chapter Six

The Ballet Rambert

The letter arrived, informing Julie of her starting date, equipment required and who to report to on the first morning of her arrival at Rambert. Her mother was excited for her daughter; her father indifferent, although there were the occasional flashes of pride in his eyes.

As she was greeted by that misty, grey Autumnal morning in 1973, she knew the effort and hardship of having to go without holidays, new clothes and even toys at Christmas, would be well worth the sacrifices made, she would make sure of that. Doreen Felix wished her well as she left her parents' home, carrying her ballet bag over one shoulder, containing her whole life; leotards, tights, pointes, flat and character shoes, not forgetting a pair of leg warmers and of course, the packed lunch her mother had prepared for her. She jumped on a tube to Nottinghill Gate and slowly, nervously walked up the Portobella Road towards Kensington Park Road, in which the Mercury Theatre was located and Ballet Rambert housed.

She stopped and stood for a moment, gazing across at the double doors, which were closed shut in similar fashion to the gateway of the Forbidden City. Shivers ran down her spine, her stomach churned, yet still she waited, scrutinising the outside of the building, waiting for her mind to regain its orderly pattern of thinking. Get in there girl and break through into your new, exciting life.

The theatre had been built as early as 1851, being extensively used for public performances and seating about 150 paying customers. In 1933, Ashley Dukes reopened the same building as the Mercury Theatre for the production of new drama and it was then that his wife, Dame Marie Rambert transformed it into the Ballet School.

When Julie first stepped through those double doors, she felt as if the ghosts of the past were all gathered there, watching her every movement. It was dark inside, with wood panelled walls and floors. The air was musty, the smell was old and damp with a hint of stale perfume. The interior was close, almost claustrophobic, but strangely she felt an unusual kind of warmth, home from home, the kind of warmth that would be an ideal environment for hard work and the kind of dedication she was so hell bent on displaying by the ton.

A small office was situated on her left and she turned before slowly stepping towards its open doorway. After being asked her name, more forms were handed over for completion. A brief meeting with the other twenty four fresh faced beginners, two thirds being girls and the remainder boys, were followed by an escort up two flights of stairs to the changing rooms. When she reached the first landing she couldn't help but admire a large pane of window glass that allowed light on to the stairs.

The changing rooms had the same ancient and plain appearance as did the rest of the building's interior. There were plastered walls with clothes pegs looking down upon wooden benches, put to good use by the students getting changed. They were all then told to gather for their first lesson in the dance studio on the ground floor.

Angela Ellis gave the students an introductory talk, telling them, "This will not be an easy ride for any of you. You are here because of your talent and we expect you to give it your all."

Julie felt in awe of the school's director and main ballet teacher, but although Miss Ellis's outward no nonsense appearance gave the impression of a harsh approach to discipline, she soon discovered that the founder's daughter was easily approachable and would later become a confidante. The other two members of staff were then introduced, Mrs. Kelly was responsible for character and contemporary dance and Miss Monroe taught ballet technique.

The dancing classes soon got under way and as the first few days past by, the daily routine became clearer. Each morning the class had to be in attendance for nine o'clock, although most mornings Julie arrived earlier for warm up exercises, feeling fresh and wanting to get every last benefit from every lesson. The first class was always the ballet lesson where the students would warm up at the ballet barre, supports attached to every wall of the studio, set against floor to ceiling mirrors. Then came centre practice with battlement tendus, involving brushing the foot along the floor, through the balls of the feet and ending in a point, each step being supervised by a teacher. That was followed by plies, movements in which the knees are bent while the back remains straight.

Each day was full and Julie's eyes constantly glistened with a formidable willingness to learn all she was taught. Her three year course at Ballet Rambert were to be the best days of her life and the feeling of total fulfillment and pleasure never left her.

She would return home each evening, bearing witness to her mother's horror at the sight of red raw open blisters on all ten of her daughter's toes. Salt water and surgical spirits were used to accelerate the healing process, but the girl from Rambert dismissed all pain and discomfort, remaining joyous at the prospect of yet another day spent learning more ballet techniques.

Julie felt like a sailor, having been given twenty five lashes at sea and then subjected to salt being rubbed into the open wounds. Again, the ferocious pain mattered not, as long as it assisted the healing process, so she could return to the school the following day, eating, living and breathing her chosen profession.

Every morning greeted her with aching limbs and a groaning body, as her feet would touch the small carpet at the side of her bed. During those early days, her routine was always the same, beginning with an inspection of her blistered feet, happy that her wounds were drying out and slowly healing.

Often she would dance on pointe with both feet bleeding, but remained determined to become the best student at Rambert. Such preparation of her mind and body was to stand her in good stead for the remainder of her professional life.

Early into that first year at Rambert, an unexpected disaster struck one of their number. A girl student, Jane, turned up one morning wearing a pair of new heavy platform boots. They were obviously the young girl's pride and joy and no one in the world was going to take them from her, except of course during lessons. Every last penny she'd managed to save had gone into those boots and she showed them off to just about everybody at the school.

As the group stepped out of the changing room, Jane's new boots were still on her feet, taking each downward step with not a care in the world. Nancy Sinatra would have been proud to have seen this girl walking to the rhythmic beat of 'These boots were made for walking.' But alas, as she reached the landing, the inevitable happened and Jane fell, pushing her arm through the large window pane.

Blood jettisoned out like water from a fireman's hose, covering both window frame and landing floorboards. The girl screamed and Julie, who was standing immediately behind thought at first that Jane had cut an artery, which wasn't that far away from the truth. Yelling for someone to call an ambulance, she grabbed Jane's injured wrist, covering herself with the girl's blood and quickly elevating it skywards, squeezing tightly in an effort to stop the haemorrhaging. By the time the ambulance arrived, Jane had gone into shock and her face ashen, losing consciousness by the second. Yet, still Julie held on, gripping as tightly as she possibly could until some initial First Aid was given by the ambulance crew and before she went with the girl to hospital, having saved her life.

Eventually, a few days later, Jane returned to the school and continued with her course, but her commitment was never the same. As for the heavy platform boots, no one ever clapped eyes on them again with apologies, of course, to Nancy Sinatra.

On one other occasion, another of the girls complained that her bust was too large for the kind of dancing techniques she was undertaking.

So, the same student decided to undergo surgery for a breast reduction, albeit, against the advice of the Rambert staff. When she returned to the school, following her cosmetic operation, a total weight of two pounds had been removed from each of her boobs, more than you would find on a butcher's slab. In fact, she had been transformed from the requirements of a dame in a pantomime to those of an agile, sleek, flat chested ballerina.

However, there was another problem; sadly, the girl with the self-inflicted flat chest quickly discovered that an imbalance of her posture had resulted and her difficulties in technique training increased tenfold. Eventually, the girl left the school of her own accord, unable to continue and knowing she'd probably gone over the top, just a little bit.

Julie developed a close friendship with another girl, Mary, who had the same mental attitude and commitment to the Dance as did the black girl from Ealing. During their lunch breaks the two girls would disappear down into the basement, a cold, dark, damp place with one heavy old green patterned couch being the central attraction.

They would share their packed lunches, provided by their mother's and then get to work. One girl would sit with her spine pressing against the back of the old green couch with both legs spread out, feet touching the wall. The other girl would then begin to push the couch forward, slowly pressing her friend closer to the wall, as her legs would stretch further. There was the odd occasion when the air would turn blue and the girl being pushed against the wall would scream out, "That's enough, I'm in bloody agony," but they had both agreed, no matter what the consequences, that couch wouldn't stop moving forward, like some kind of instrument of torture seen in those Vincent Price horror movies, until the exercise had been completed and the 'Box Split' accomplished.

Another exercise the dancers were committed to in their preparation was known as the 'fouette rond de jambe en tournant' which is an action whereby the individual has to stand motionless on one flat foot, bending the knee as the other leg is turned around the side, resulting in one full revolution or spin of the body. The movement was first introduced in 1893 by Pierina Legnani in Cinderella performed in St Petersburg. Legnani actually performed thirty two fouettes without stopping and without moving an inch. The ability to complete thirty two fouettes is called a bravura step, designed to test the stamina and technique of the dancer. And that is the reason why every student at the Ballet Rambert was required to repeat Legnani's nineteenth century legendary performance.

On other lunch breaks, Julie and Mary would return to the studio and practice pointe work, concentrating on fouettes, both girls determined to reach that magical number of thirty two. Unknown to them at that time, Angela Ellis was never too far away and became more and more impressed by these two particular girls who seemed to have an endless reservoir of stored up energy and commitment.

That same energy and commitment, coupled with the exhaustion and pain they shared, tended to draw Julie and Mary closer together. For Julie, it was all about the Mallory Towers series of books she had read, hoping that one day she would experience the same kind of bonding friendship the kids in the books enjoyed, having been subjected to so much isolation during her childhood years. Of course, she knew only too well that Mary was her main competitor, in fact the only competitor she had, but was still her best friend, a like-minded friend who was quite happy to devour half of Julie's lunch pack.

The excitement of her life used to be toned down a peg or two whenever the school holidays came along and the Ballet Rambert closed for respite and preparation for the next term. No dancing for Julie meant there would be no friends, which meant she had no life, albeit temporarily. Mary lived some distance away and as for her old school friends who she would occasionally bump into, they were still dismissive of her, still showing their rejection because she was black. She absolutely hated not being able to go to the dance school and appreciated the magic of Rambert, where there were no problems regarding the colour of her skin, which gave her the kind of happiness she had always been so desperately seeking, no one mentioning the fact she was black. At Rambert, it wasn't important.

Her parents couldn't afford a holiday because all of their money was being spent on Julie's ballet training. So, during those holidays of inactivity, she would catch the same early morning tube to Nottinghill Gate, walk along the Portobella Road until she reached the school. Then she would just stand there, sometimes for a few minutes, sometimes even longer, yearning for those double doors to reopen and for classes to re-commence. Her mental attitude was similar to that of a jilted lover, pining for the man who had turned his back on her. That was a measure of the depth of commitment and dedication she had for her profession. If only she could jump into one of those Mallory Towers books and become wrapped up in the adventures portrayed in between the pages.

By the end of her first six months at Rambert, she had matured considerably, her outlook on life in general and in particular, the harsh training schedule she had to endure, widened beyond expectation. It had been a period of her life in which, for the first time, she had been accepted by others for what she was and equal amongst white friends. New optimism, self-confidence and perhaps above all, the feeling that she was a human being standing on a level plain with everyone else. They were all there to become professional dancers and as far as Julie was concerned, the ballet experience had developed into a pulsating and real achievement. As soon as those double doors reopened, she would be there with her glistening eyes and broad wonderful smile, which had also developed beyond expectation.

Chapter Seven

Outside Influences

'It is possible, I think, to make the audience believe you are a distraught Juliet by the way you move your body alone'.

It is insufficient for the dance student to just feel emotion within themselves; they must be capable of transporting that same emotion to the audience. To steal Barbara Hepworth's philosophy about carving in stone being an interrelated mass conveying an emotion, Classical Ballet requires similar elements. A perfect relationship between the mind and the dance, which is projected from the performance to the audience.

To achieve such captivation requires a whole network of methods, movement of the body, arms and hands, or the sensitivity and positioning of the eyes. But above all, the dancer must firstly feel emotion, whether sadness, joy, love or anger, inside their very soul and there is no better way to build a bank of such feelings than real life experiences.

During her first year at Rambert, Julie quickly realised that her intensive feeling and love for ballet dancing, would never be sufficient to reach the high standard she was attempting to achieve. Dance technique and development alone were insufficient. They were only aspects of personal life changes to attitude and something deeper had to be reached when it came to Classical Ballet. For example, when a dancer moves back from her partner, at the same time portraying anger or sadness, then in order to convince the audience that such emotions are being felt, the same emotions must be genuinely present in the dancer's mind and projected in a true, realistic manner.

Although Julie's full time commitment to her cause left little time for relationships and boyfriends, she was conscious of the necessity to widen her perspectives and personal life in general. To build a bank of inward emotions, which was necessary to progress. It was difficult to maintain friendships outside the ballet school, but occasionally she would visit a public house or other social haunt with her sister, Lucia, just to try and catch snippets of gossip from local people chattering away over their drinks. Sometimes she would just sit there, next to Lucia, watching, observing others and listening to various conversations, at the same time, learning.

Julie had always looked up to Lucia, and the two sisters shared most things, except their own personal visions for the future. At the same time she was working hard, practicing and rehearsing at dancing lessons, her older sister was planning for a life far different. After leaving school, Lucia went to Twickenham College to study 'A' level Art before being employed as a Layout Artist by Conde Nast, a New York magazine publications company based in London. She stayed there for a few years before acknowledging there was no possibility of further advancement. She began to feel stale, realising the need for greater challenges to feed her imaginative and adventurous mind, so decided to leave after taking an interest in cooking. Although she never gained any cooking qualifications, her determination and personality landed Lucia with a job as a personal chef to the newly discovered pop group, 'Take That'.

After a short period she moved on again, seeking and obtaining employment with the BBC, where she gained further experience as a chef with the production staff of the Tele Tubbies projects. But the initial excitement soon dwindled and she began to miss the travel aspects of her previous job with 'Take That'. Lucia was successful in applying for a job as a travel representative with the travel company Thomson and soon found herself working as a travel guide on the Greek Island of Zakynthos, where she quickly fell in love with a local boy who was full of ideas about what their future might hold.

She gave Thomson's her notice and together with her new found Greek love, bought a small beach restaurant on Zakynthos, which initially brought some financial success. But all that was to yet to come.

Falling in love had never entered Lucia's younger sister's mind and Julie was well aware that such an emotion didn't come at the press of a button. Cupid's arrow had to strike naturally, possibly never, possibly once a day or once a week, or once in a lifetime. No matter, her intention wasn't to find love but to understand it more, so she could interpret the same in her dance routines. She was naïve when it came to relationships and felt an overwhelming desire to improve that weakness.

She met her first boyfriend, a Welsh lad by the name of Keith, during one of her excursions to a local inn. They soon began to converse, as most couples initially do, in easy chat and rapport, until Julie's profession became clear and unsurprisingly, the centre of their conversation for the rest of the evening. In similar fashion to suddenly finding out the person you were conversing with was in fact a trained fighter pilot, with an allocated location in an enemy country which had to be destroyed if the order was ever given, the boy became just as fascinated by Julie's rare lifestyle, commitment and unswerving dedication.

He was an electrician, which meant there was no contest when it came to discussing their vastly different vocations. In fairness to Keith, a conversation about the wiring of a house or factory, or high voltage cables or aluminium alloy conductors, could never be as magnetic as probing rudimentary and basic requirements involved in ballet training.

But a mutual liking between the two youngsters became apparent and they started to date, with Julie feeling proud that a white boy had somehow become interested in her.

It didn't take long for Julie's maturity and inquisitiveness about the rest of the world to surface. She was only being honest with herself in the belief that a boyfriend would help to develop her career even further. Of course, such presumption was selfish but with this girl, it was synonymous with the kind of dedication and deep affection she had for her profession. However, when the topic of conversation between the two romantics frequently focused on red raw open blisters and toes and blood seeping through ballet shoes, she often wondered whether she had gone down the right path. Poor old Keith the electrician!

Apart from Julie's father taking to the young Welsh kid, there wasn't any other really positive thing that came from their relationship. There was the girlfriend, constantly talking about her passion for ballet, her aching body, exhaustion and those bloody blisters which always seemed to dominate her feet, and the poor old boyfriend, sitting in awe of everything his girl was verbally sharing with him, mouth open and eyes just staring back at her. You didn't have to be a super sleuth to realise that their relationship would soon be under pressure. But, as if determined to show this girl that her career difficulties mattered not to him, he presented Julie with an engagement ring.

Keith had waited his opportunity until they had left the cinema and were both walking towards Julie's bus stop, where he would see her catch her bus home, before disappearing into the night air. Well, on this particular occasion and while Julie was wondering why they were having to walk so slowly, worried that she would miss that bus, he suddenly stopped to face her. Producing the ring from a tight fitting pocket, he placed it on her finger and smiled.

Julie responded with a wide appreciative grin and those same glistening black eyes, only witnessed when she was inside the Ballet Rambert. She stood like a beautiful swan, waiting at the lakeside in anticipation for the arrival of her handsome Cob.

"I hope you like it?" Keith said.

"I do, it's beautiful," answered Julie, "Thank you."

Then the bus came.

The problem Keith had was he never made it clear whether the ring was a sign of his intention to marry the girl, or at least ask for her hand. Or, whether his purchase was intended just to seal their relationship. In fact, that information was never forthcoming.

The couple continued to meet but over the next few weeks, Julie's love for her art grew more and more. The emotions she was experiencing for the ballet were beginning to outweigh the emotions she was feeling towards Keith. So, decision time came like a bolt out of the blue, in similar fashion to Lucia's later decision to go halves in a beach restaurant on a Greek Island. Having decided it was unfair to continue a relationship which she regarded as being unfaithful to her secret lover existing in the wings of her relationship with Keith, she called time on their relationship and Keith was never seen again, having taken back his ring, of course.

Ballet was her true love, her real companion and Julie's only confidante at that particular time of her young life, which meant there could be no room for a second adoration, and that's what Keith had been, secondary to her first and only obsession. There were no tears, no argument and she continued to socialise 'around town' with her beloved sister. On occasions, the two girls would be found either in a local public house, or Kensington High Street where the Biba shop was located. Arm in arm, they spent hours sifting through rails of clothes, casting their eyes over every trinket and other enticing items that appealed to most girls of their age, advertised in exchange for ready cash. Of course, there was no intention of buying anything, there was no money, but wishful thinking never hurt anyone.

Most of whatever Julie had in monetary gain would be spent on dance clothing or the occasional hot chocolate. Lucia's money was always used to purchase alcohol. Yet they were sisters, loyal friends, a couple who shared the kind of love and respect only sisters could. They were a team together; they were the best and hung out together as much as they could.

The ballet dancer always admired her sister's wisdom, except when it came to drink, and respected the mature, infectiously calm attitude Lucia was blessed with. She adored her older sister's vivacious personality, which shone like a large beacon illuminating a forest floor covered with motionless bluebells at night. She was still the withdrawn kid, when in Lucia's presence, but remained the same girl who had no equal for sparkling and spirited performances once on stage and beneath the lights which heated her black skin. Once however, the pointe shoes had been stored away, her true personality was there for all to see, mild mannered and the epitome of shyness.

Chapter Eight

Technique

As she reached her nineteenth birthday and began her second year at Rambert, Julie's life in general became more settled. The daily rides on the underground saw the girl becoming more smug and indifferent to those other travellers who sat and stood around her. One of her driving forces was the belief she was more special than any other member of the human race, including other dancers. She was a black ballet dancer on the road to greatness and before long the whole world would become aware of the artistic talents of one Julie Felix.

As the tube swayed from side to side, racing between underground stations, she would stand upright, jostling with the movement of the train, testing her balance, practicing her adage for the ballet lesson which awaited her arrival at Nottinghill Gate, transferring her weight from one foot to the other, as she had been taught during every glorious day at the school.

Of course, balance was a major key, but controlled balance was the end result of hours of practice and that could very useful when rattling along on the London Underground on a tube being driven by a person who didn't give a toss about whether passengers were flight of foot and well balanced. This self-styled routine continued throughout most of her second year at Rambert though, and the yearning for greater life experience had diminished. That was until one day, the early morning tube train was unusually quiet and for once, she managed to conquer a seat.

As the transport raced through the tunnels towards her destination, Julie's thoughts were empty, gone to sleep, concentrating on nothing in particular. It was going to be one of those days. Then she suddenly noticed a stranger standing nearby, swaying with the train's movements, staring directly at her. One thing she didn't notice was that the Ginger Tom, with a pale face and unholy smirk across his face, was wearing the accustomed gabardine mackintosh, the one that's usually two sizes too big and denotes the presence of an undercover cop or pervert. Having nothing better to do, fantasy came to her rescue and she momentarily believed the balding, ginger haired man with the smirk had recognised her for being a world famous ballerina, from the way she had walked into the carriage, gliding with a straight back and feet turned outwards, the perfect posture maintained at all times.

Her imaginative bubble suddenly burst when the train stopped at the next station and to Julie's horror and surprise, the ginger ninja suddenly opened his raincoat and fully exposed himself to the potential ballerina. He then turned and casually stepped through the open doors, leaving behind a bewildered and very surprised young girl. The fact the flasher hadn't presented too much on his plate of disgust, nothing more than a maggot and two peas, didn't help the state of shock she went into.

When she finally arrived at Rambert that morning, she was still well outside her normal state of calmness and control and related the details of her latest life experience to the staff. They sat Julie down with a drink of water and asked, obviously concerned, if she was okay to continue with the day's lessons and of course she replied in the positive. All she could think of was how she could use that most recent experience to develop her inward emotions when later dancing, although the picture that had earlier been flashed to her by Ginger Tom could have been more magnetic. It hadn't exactly been the kind that would have turned the smallest alley cat into a sex seeking feline maniac. But there again, it had sufficed enough to help her grow up some and that particular incident hadn't just landed on her doorstep as a result of turning the sound up.

Julie's crusade continued and the fascination she had with the mechanics of the human body and how its movements worked, propelling even the most graceless people in everyday life, was compelling and in some way, challenging, provided she didn't break a leg. Understanding the fact that a specific movement could create the most beautiful position and be regarded as a work of art, helped her to progress further.

Sandwiched in between classes both Julie and Mary would find some place to do more rigorous training. Extra exercises, pointe work, more of the infamous fouettes or old green couch stretches down in the basement, screaming their heads off as their stomachs touched the wall. The girls were like two fillies with the bits in their mouths, chasing towards the finishing line, but not really wanting the finishing line to come into view.

As an advanced student, she appreciated the huge amount of effort and hard work the dancer had to put in to make the ballet look effortless, was beyond the comprehension of most ordinary people. Understanding the conflict between body and requirement also helped. Since childhood, she had been entwined in a battle against the opposition quandary, the opposition being the racist taunts and acknowledgements, which was the reason she felt The Ballet so well. Her dancing unchained her, elevating the mind and expectations far above the restrictions which she felt when she was away from Rambert.

It became obvious that Angela Ellis knew she had something special in this particular student, by the way she constantly studied Julie in training, but that didn't stop her from yelling out, "Don't lean on the barre, Julie," from a corner of the studio. At least Julie got some comfort from knowing the school director was watching her, and loved her for it.

Tendu exercises were necessary to warm up and stretch the feet in a tight crossed legged position called the fifth position, the fundamental basis of all of the ballet technique. Turned out, rotated hips and legs and feet, in that order. The man on the train, Ginger Tom, would have loved this lot.

Safety was the key issue as far as Julie was concerned, having read and heard about how easy it was to suffer injuries. She was well aware that if you took good care of the body that's been given to you, then it would serve you for as long as the passion remained inside. When the passion died, so did the dancer.

Other exercises included the glisse or jete, which is a progression of the tendu, slightly lifting the leg higher, shooting the leg away from the body, like a bullet being fired from a gun, encouraged precision and speed taking control. In order to open the hips, the student needed to make ronde de jambe, meaning round of the leg, which involved circles of the legs like the dot to dot puzzle where a pencil line has to be drawn from point one to two, to three and so on. And all completed en dehors and en de dans, meaning outwards and inwards. It was such a bloody pity she hadn't used these techniques on Ginger Tom, by kicking him where it hurt most, before he made good his escape.

Finally, the exercises would be completed with Grand battemans, big kicks of the legs and once they have been done away with, time to get off that barre and use all that had been practiced to dance.

So, why the hell does a person want to get involved in ballet? Is it for the love of dancing, the gruelling and physical training that goes with it, or the pretty tu-tu's they wear? Julie's reason was to prove everyone wrong; to become engaged in the wars between different cultures, colours and passions; to become Britain's first black ballerina.

The biggest can of worms for the male members to overcome was the insistence they never dropped their partners. If a boy committed such a cardinal sin, the consequences just fell short of being dragged off to meet Madame Guillotine, it would certainly result in a fate far worse than death itself, after being constantly reminded by the director, Angela Ellis, that under no circumstances would they drop their female partner. The demand to do everything in their power to prevent such a catastrophe from happening was constantly drummed into them.

Then one day the inevitable happened and there stood the shamed boy, in the centre of the studio, glaring down in despair and horror at the young female elfin creature he'd just allowed to slip from his supporting arms, to the floor. The outcome was the kind of riotous commotion that could have been heard back at the underground tube station, where Julie's flasher lurked with his gabardine mackintosh still open for anyone willing to be insulted. Luckily for the young culprit in the studio, only his pride was hurt, but the bawling out he received would be remembered for the remainder of his life.

All remained settled at home with Julie enjoying the freedom bestowed on her by her parents, although her father was still making the odd grumble and the family budget feeling the strain from the bills that came in from Rambert.

"Just look at him," her mother would say, "Everywhere he goes, he smiles at people, charms and interests them, but as soon as he walks through that front door of his, the face on him changes dramatically. You could use it to scare the local kids off from jumping in the canal."

Julie would smile, appreciating that most married couples had their differences, even when one was white and the other black. Patrick Felix had swallowed his fair bit of racism though, but had still continued to work hard for his family, and his youngest daughter loved him for it. One day she would make him proud, of that she was certain. One day he would look upon his girl as if she'd just found gold in California, sweeping away all the financial problems that were giving him sleepless nights.

The teaching and learning continued with Julie constantly stretching her capabilities to the limit, seeking a further, greater limit, her mind constantly full of all she had learned from her classes. Her secret love affair was as strong as ever, perhaps even stronger as each day and each lesson went by. New challenges, awesome and testing challenges were cast her way each time she stepped into class, but she relished every fresh idea, every new method and felt the progress she was making oozing throughout her inner soul. If only that pervert had known what kind of devastating human fitness machine he was flashing his tea and sugar at.

'All that matters is love and work' Freud

Chapter Nine

Julie's Rejection

The 1975 summer break from training held a different flavour for Julie because she'd decided it was time to help her parents out with some extra cash. Most of what mum and dad had been earning went towards supporting their daughter's ambitions. So, having received the news there was a new kid on the block, McDonald's having opened their first business premises in the country, off she went down to Kensington High Street and got herself a job with a load of other kids.

It was all very new and at first, a little bewildering for the trainee ballet dancer. She felt as if she'd been suddenly dropped into the middle of an important race to see who could serve more customers quicker than anyone else. But Julie with the spinning head, enjoyed the work and enjoyed the money she earned even more.

After a few days she caught the eye of a boy who visited the burger bar on a couple of occasions, before a few courteous words were exchanged. Finally, the lad asked Julie for a date, after telling her his name was Kevin and he'd come up to London from Cornwall. With a smile on her face, she agreed to go out with him but on one condition, he didn't try to charm her by buying a hamburger!

The Electric Cinema was beckoning and they went to see the film, 'The Rocky Horror Show,' where staff members appeared out of the woodwork dressed in similar clothing to those characters in the film. It was all good fun and Julie quickly found out that Kevin shared some of her interests in the arts. Obviously, like Keith before him, he became fascinated by his new girlfriend's profession, but the connection was there and a common interest helped the relationship along its merry, romantic way.

After a while, the young couple became very close and on this occasion she wasn't going with Kevin just to improve her social experiences. He eventually invited Julie to visit Truro with him to meet his parents. She'd always enjoyed going to the 'seaside' and the visit brought back memories of her father's old Ford Zodiac, in which the family used to go for a day out every other Sunday to Bognor Regis, with her mother behind the wheel because dad couldn't drive and Doreen Felix had learned when driving lorries in the WAFs during the war. Anyway, Kevin's parents took to their son's new girlfriend and she wondered whether they would ask where she had got her fabulous tan from, but they didn't and Julie's relationship with the Truro lad got stronger, although there was a particular surprise package waiting to test her resilience.

Kevin introduced her to something totally different to anything she'd ever experienced before, shark fishing. As the small boat pulled away from the quay the water remained calm as a result of shelter from the harbour wall, but as soon as the craft hit the open sea a gale force eight came down on the fisher folk and the boat began to leap up and down like a demented cork.

"Shall we be heading back now Kevin?" Julie asked, only having left Truro a matter of minutes before, feeling her stomach beginning to churn and having to retain a hold on any part of the boat that was solid to prevent herself from going overboard.

"We're okay for a bit yet," Kevin snapped back, much to the trainee ballerina's despair, "The skipper reckons this one will blow over pretty soon."

Now the only problem with being sea sick is that you stay sea sick until you get your feet back on hard dry land. In the meantime the poor affected soul has to endure a nightmare of nauseating sensations. One other aspect of having your stomach dominate your movements when bobbing up and down, is that it also pays to take note of which way the wind is blowing and that particular failure was unfortunately the downfall of Julie.

As she wrenched with her head hanging over the side, she happened to turn towards the front of the boat and all that once belonged to her stomach was blown straight back, leaving the girl sitting down covered in that morning's breakfast. She couldn't scream out because she was too ill and the second course was already making its way up towards her mouth. The aged skipper, who owned the boat and was both helmsman and navigator, suddenly appeared and threw a bucket full of sea water all over the front of Julie, covering the girl from head to waist.

"Aye, that should do it lass, now you rest up a while," the man in charge suggested.

"Thank you," she gasped in answer, pretty pissed off, sitting there with her hair full of salt water and her whole upper torso dripping wet.

The only thing Julie wanted to do at that moment was die a thousand deaths. But, apart from that unfortunate incident, all in all, it wasn't a bad summer break that year.

When the third year at Rambert loomed on the horizon, Julie decided to remain at McDonalds, working every Wednesday evening and Saturday. She stayed there for about a year, intending to remain until her training at Rambert had been concluded. After all, it was helping her parents' financial difficulties.

The third and final year was no pushover: forget the business about putting on the final coat of polish, the students quickly found it to be even more intensive than the previous year. Their routine was basically the same as before, but at a higher tempo. A huge amount of preparation was also injected into the schedule, aimed towards gaining an apprenticeship with a dance company. Curriculum Vitas were compiled under supervision and once they had been completed, a list of leading ballet companies in England and Europe were provided for the students to post off their photographs and personal documents, once they felt they were ready for the outside world. Of course there was no such thing in those days as digital photographs or pictures, which meant there could be no hair brushing for improvements. What the viewer saw, the viewer got.

During that same year, Julie discovered a well-known American company, the Dance Theatre Harlem, had been nominated to appear in that year's Royal Command Performance at the London Palladium. She was tracked down by an old childhood friend, another black girl by the name of Brenda, who actually worked for the Harlem dancers. Brenda suggested she could arrange for Julie to have a company class, under the watchful eye of the company's founder and director, Arthur Mitchell, the first black ballet dancer ever to perform publicly in America.

Julie realised that the company class would in fact be an audition and the notion of performing for an American group didn't impress her. The truth was, she had no intention at that time of working in any other country except England. She had always intended to prove all of those doubters in her earlier years wrong and was hell bent on working for a British ballet company. But, Brenda was insistent and finally arranged, through Arthur Mitchell, for Julie to attend.

It was on a Friday when she arrived at the stage door of the London Palladium with her ballet bag over one shoulder and her nerve endings doing their usual twitching trick. The feeling of guilt at not having told Angela Ellis about the audition, didn't help much either. After being ushered into the changing rooms Julie found herself being warmly welcomed by the professionals who had travelled from Harlem for the performance. They managed to calm her nerves by talking to her as if she was a long lost friend, making her feel she was welcome and at home, which seemed strange to her, being as they were the foreigners visiting her country.

She was also surprised to discover that many of those male and female black ballet dancers had also suffered rejection because of the colour of their skin, in similar fashion to what she had experienced. At least they all had something in common with the Rambert girl and admired and respected Arthur Mitchell for having given them a chance with Harlem. It was a warming experience for Julie, who enjoyed chatting away to them on the same level.

Memories of all the auditions she'd had, before seeking the sanctuary of Rambert came flooding back to her. The shaky nerves, anxiety and tweaking stomachs, but above all she couldn't forget and never would, the rejections and reason for those rejections.

She met Arthur Mitchell and they both shook hands. It was ironic, the first female black ballet dancer in the United Kingdom meeting up with the first black ballet dancer in the United States. She felt proud, but still extremely nervous.

Other artists due to appear on the same bill and with whom she brushed shoulders included, Lionel Blair, Tom O'Connor, Max Bygraves and Shirley Bassey. Of course they were all busy rehearsing their own acts and had little time for a small, thinly built black girl, standing nearby in awe of such a collection of professional talent. That particular Royal Variety Performance was to be attended by the Queen and the Queen Mother and unknown to Julie at that time, it was to be the first RVP ever to be televised live.

Finally she managed to return to earth and shed those damned fears. As if spurred on by that gathering of people at the top of their profession, she danced and danced, throwing everything in she had learned and developed over the previous two years. Once again, she skipped and moved, as though her life depended on it and when she came to the end of her performance, received some encouraging applause from the rest of the company who'd been watching from the wings. Arthur Mitchell offered her a twelve month contract, even before she had left the floor.

Julie even amazed herself when she heard her own words refusing the contract offered. Mitchell just shrugged his shoulders, bewildered by this young black girl's audacity, before he casually walked away, obviously wondering to himself what the hell was that all about? Why had the girl auditioned in the first place?

As for Julie, well she just picked up her ballet bag and left the theatre. Her rebuff had resulted from those same strong principles which had driven her throughout her time at Rambert. Her own future plans and professional path were carved in stone and the strength of her character guaranteed there would be no movement away from her ambitions and intentions. That inner personal vault was filled with the same kind of deep commitment that had pushed her to near perfection when dancing and had seen her through all the pain and hardship that went with it. So, by hook or by crook, the girl was going to show the doubting Brits they had been wrong. A black girl could dance as well, if not much better than any other dancer, in The Ballet.

Throughout that weekend, she despaired, her inner self telling her that she had made a dreadful mistake. Or had she? Was it right for a black girl, living and working in the kind of elite community which enveloped Classical Ballet, to turn down any opportunity? Had she finally lost her way as a result of her principles, no matter how strong they were? She would soon find out one way or another.

The following Monday, she returned to Rambert and the first thing she did was tell Angela Ellis all about what she had done with the Harlem Company, trying to explain her reasons for turning down the offer of a contract. Miss Ellis took a deep breath which was followed by an outburst that bounced off every wall in the school, as her heavy jewellery shook like the ground above an earthquake.

"Darling," she bawled out, "I cannot believe you have turned down a contract with one as prestigious as the Harlem Dance Company." Fires blazed in the director's eyes as she continued, "Whatever were you thinking of? No one turns down a contract."

It seemed that all the egotism and pompous attitudes the girl had fought against all her life had suddenly taken over Julie. Who the hell did she think she was? A veil of shame descended upon her like a fire curtain falling. It was with a heavy heart she realised she had let her ballet teacher down, badly. Her new fear was that Angela Ellis would now reject her, perhaps even throw her out of Rambert. For a pupil, barely into her third year at the school, to be offered a job was a rarity. The kudos the school would have gained at such an achievement would have been huge.

Then there were her parents, still struggling to support her. Had she let them down as well? Of course she had and with all the pain she had felt during those hours of hard work and training, nothing compared with what she was feeling inside her heart at that particular moment.

Not too long after that horrendous Monday at Rambert, Julie heard through the grapevine that the Dance Theatre Harlem had left the country and flown back to the States, taking with them, the girl's chance of ever being offered a professional ballet contract with them. She was in bits and cried torrents, repeatedly asking the same question. 'What in God's name have I done?'

For two weeks she remained completely off course. The old green couch down in the basement no longer called to her for the usual joyous punishment and Mary had to fouette alone. Even Kevin's daily offer of a hot chocolate after school, having replaced Mary's long standing duty, failed to console her broken heart. Would she ever come to terms ever again with the belief her true secret lover had abandoned her?

Chapter Ten

Rudolf Nureyev – Premiere Danceur

Julie's personal battle continued throughout that final year at Rambert and she felt she was beginning to understand more fully, the wider aspects of the business she had been embarking on. The need to identify an horizon and reach that goal, before stretching the line even further, like a climber, scaling a mountain and achieving each ridge, before finally reaching the top. But above all, her resilience had to remain strong. She often reflected on the occasions her mother would take her as a young girl and teach her how to swim. Although she always loved the water, she was never a strong swimmer and when, still only an infant, the girl's developing trust of water was challenged unmercifully.

Her sister had a friend, who often boasted on the length she could slice through the water, without her feet touching the floor. One day, she told Julie to sit on her shoulders, which the naïve small girl did, her sister's friend holding both arms. Slowly the self-professed channel swimmer then began to walk up the centre of the Ealing Swimming Bath, towards the deep end. As she did, carrying Julie on her shoulders, the water began to reach higher and higher until it completely covered the two girls.

Julie panicked and began to struggle, with the other girl retaining her grip on the younger girl's arms. Was that stupid or what? Certainly extremely dangerous. The infant genuinely believed she was about to leave this world, not having yet seen that many Christmas mornings. Eventually, she broke free and managed to struggle to the safety of the side of the bath, terrified and gasping for breath. She would never again place so much trust on another's intentions, but Julie had learned a valuable lesson from that trauma, one that would remain with her throughout her life. Sinking had never been an option, or so she made herself believe.

So it was, during that period of upheaval at Rambert, there was no way on earth she was going to sink now. Those bad memories of the Harlem experience at the Palladium, still haunted her. The shame she had felt wouldn't surrender and leave her, but she forged on, re-enforcing her armour and determined to hit back, stronger than ever before. She only had herself to blame and was desperate to show Angela Ellis that she would never let her down again. This was to be the new Julie. Sinking was not an option.

The change in her approach was awesome, in some ways frightening to those who bared witness. The other students could only look on in amazement as the slip of a black girl from Ealing flew around the studio, like a graceful bird in controlled flight. As she continued daily to torture herself in training, she forced her adrenaline levels to reach new heights and remained totally focused on every move she made, excelling beyond what she had never done before.

Julie raised her vibration, her very being, feeling masses of energy, frustration and anger hissing out like steam from a boiling kettle. She instantly absorbed everything thrown at her by the teaching staff, forever smiling as she did so. She began to see and correct others mistakes, as if experiencing some out of body wizardry. Julie was reaching far beyond her own boundaries, occupying an invisible space which was forbidden for the majority of human beings. Such inhuman achievement was being developed, not just for her own benefit, but for everybody else who looked on. Overnight she had pushed herself both mentally and physically to a standard reserved only for Olympiads.

Even Julie had never realised how great the driving force inside her young girl's body had become. Was it the self-imposed quest or crusade she had decided to conquer? Or perhaps the strength of desire to flush out all the frustrating wrongs that had plagued her over that last few weeks? In truth, it was both. She had soared through the air on the swings at the local park when a young girl; she had jumped higher in the studio than she could ever have imagined. But now, she was flying again, showing off both to others and herself. Julie was the best and no one, no one would be able to deny that ever again.

As the months continued, so did Julie's determination to stay at the top of the class. Her constant improvements in ballet technique continued to climb, right through the top of the barometer, until finally, Angela Ellis, threw a gift to this audacious and daredevil girl, the greatest reward possible for a third year student at Rambert.

It was another lunchtime break which saw Julie and Mary back in the basement, keeping the old green couch company. The room had been turned into a shambles, something that resembled a bombed out living room, with pointe and other ballet shoes, tops, leg warmers and just about every other type of clothing and equipment you could imagine, strewn about the place, in such a way, the girls hadn't seen the floor for weeks. After all, this had become Julie and Mary's room, their haven and their sanctuary.

The girl from Ealing was completely jacked up against the wall, back pressing against the couch with her face just an inch or two away from the plaster, just enough to enable her head to rotate sufficiently to eat a sandwich. Mary of course, was in attendance, guaranteeing Julie's position remained static and pushing that bloody green couch even more so towards the wall. The scene was set and that's exactly what greeted Angela Ellis as she entered the basement room.

Well, at first only Mary saw the director standing there at the bottom of the stairs with a stern look across her face. She leapt from the couch, causing Julie to fall slightly back from the wall. A struggle then followed and Mrs. Ellis had to wait, while her favourite student untangled herself before getting to her feet, with strands of hair hanging down over her face and soft blasphemy coming from her mouth, targeting Mary for having allowed the couch to slide back. It was only then she saw Angela Ellis and immediately believed she was about to be crucified.

Miss Ellis waited to allow a short period of settling silence fill the room. Her eyes sparkled like Julie had never noticed before, and then she gave the girls the news. Remaining where she stood, obviously in fear of tripping over any of the multitude of items scattered around the floor, she explained that The London Festival Ballet was putting on Nureyev's production of Sleeping Beauty at the London Coliseum. The director was Dame Beryl Gray.

Julie's mind went into overdrive. Why tell them all this? Was Mrs. Ellis going to offer them free tickets or perhaps the opportunity to watch the great Rudolf Nureyev in rehearsal? What an experience that would be. But then, as if deliberately speaking slowly, enjoying the look of anticipation on both girls faces, the lady explained, "Dame Beryl has asked for two dancers from Rambert to be used as extras to perform with the company and I want you both to take part in this great performance."

"To dance with Nureyev?" Julie asked, unable to conceal the disbelief and astonishment in her shaky voice.

"Yes, I have no doubt you will both be in the corps de ballet supporting Mr. Nureyev."

Both girls turned and faced each other, shaking and giggling with excitement, their ballet shoes hitting the stone floor like machine gun fire. Christmas had come early for them and they only diverted their eyes away from each other when they heard Angela Ellis climbing back up the stairs.

After school Julie couldn't get home quick enough to tell her mother of her good fortune. Good fortune? She had left Planet Earth and was now thoughtless, trembling with joy and every other emotion indulged in when a child meets Santa Claus in real life for the first time. There was no flasher in the world could have attracted Julie's attention on that train journey home.

Once through Patrick's colourful front door, it was all spurted out with no time to think, no time to even breathe, just a torrent of excited and joyous verbal communication. Her mother listened with incredulity, her eyes filling with tears, speechless. Mom later told dad, as soon as he returned home from work and although Patrick's usual indifferent look remained his mask, deep down he was now beginning to seriously think that perhaps this daughter of his really did have the kind of talent that would bring her success and fortune.

Each morning after that, Julie woke up feeling no pain, no aching body or grumbling toes, her mind focused only on one thing, the biggest event of her life thus far. Thank you Mrs. Ellis. Thank you Dame Beryl Gray and a big thank you to his Highness, Rudolf Nureyev.

Two weeks after being told of their good fortune, the girls began rehearsals at the London Coliseum, home of the London Festival Ballet. They were given the choreography for the roles they were to perform and rehearsed with the other members of the cast, including the Prima Ballerina, Eva Evdokimova. A studio was used for the initial movements, before the same would be repeated on stage with a pianist playing the different scores. After they had been given time to rehearse, both girls from Rambert were instructed to sit quietly in a corner, watching and dreaming. Of course, both Julie and Mary had been well drilled on how to behave, they didn't speak unless spoken to, didn't get up until told to do so. They were living in a magical world, one they had only talked and read about. The only problem was, neither of them had yet set eyes on Nureyev.

Whispers began to be exchanged amongst the dancers.

"He's coming today."

"I've heard he isn't coming until tomorrow."

"I've heard he isn't coming until opening night."

"I've heard he isn't coming at all."

Then he came, like a hurricane rushing through the doors of the auditorium, with a brown, real fur coat draped across his shoulders and wearing a calf-length pair of light tan boots, which he never took off, even when marking his steps on stage. His expression was stern and without speaking, he spun his coat around his shoulders in similar fashion to a Matador rotating his cape, the world's leading Premiere Danceur's coat flew through the air and landed on the floor. Rudolf had arrived and the whole theatre immediately fell under his spell.

You could hear a pin drop as the silence almost became overbearing. All before him remained motionless, staring at this man who had already made ballet history. Both Julie and Mary felt as if they had suddenly been captured in a freeze frame and time had come to an abrupt full stop.

Dame Beryl Gray made the first move, spitting out a thousand words of welcome to the male star of the show. Those boots hadn't yet moved from where they had stood since entering the auditorium. Then this God of Classical Ballet spoke his first words for everyone to hear.

"I will take over from here." Well, you couldn't be more abrupt than that, but it was the trigger for business to kick off once again and life returned, much the same as turning on a light in a Manhattan flat and seeing all the cockroaches flying about in search of darkness.

This was to be Nureyev's version of Sleeping Beauty and although the ballet had been performed around the world many times previously, because it was his version, it automatically gave him licence to change, alter or adapt any aspect of the performance. During the next few days, the routine was always the same. He would enter, speak and then mark out his steps on the stage, remaining as long as required, which could be minutes or longer, but certainly no more than a couple of hours, before he would disappear as quickly as he'd made his entrance. Those tanned boots of his never came off by the way.

When Nureyev was present, the rehearsals always went up a gear, at neck breaking pace, and when he had left, everything slowed down once again to an easier more manageable gait.

"What happened then?"

"Was that a mirage I saw?"

"Did we really see Nureyev."

Chapter Eleven

Bitter Sweet

During the time Julie and Mary spent rehearsing at the Coliseum, they still had to return to Rambert for a daily morning class, before then leaving to continue with the London Festival Ballet. The hustle and bustle of their new found life made them yearn for the peace and quiet of that old green couch, but the day of the performance was approaching quickly.

Finally it came, with the dancers ready to give their all. At 7.0 p.m. the half hour curtain call echoed throughout the changing rooms. It was during that thirty minute period, before the curtain was raised for the first act to kick off, last minute preparations could be made. Some of the dancers continued with their warming up exercises, while others put Rosen on their pointe shoes, which prevented slipping. The tension increased with the sounds of movement and snippets of conversation on the other side of the curtain as the audience began to take their seats, and the orchestra began tuning up.

The countdown began and just before the house lights were about to dim and the stage lights go up and the curtain raised as a signal for the orchestra to turn up the volume, Julie and Mary were ordered to their dressing rooms to await their turn.

So, there they sat, listening intently to the distant spasms of applause and the orchestras changing musical themes. When their call came to make the wings, they were both feeling the pulse, but ready to give everything to the performance. When finally entering the Ballet as members of the corps de ballet, Nureyev was the lead dancer, astonishing the audience with his agility and grace. The Royal Gala was the first of many festivals that followed at the London Coliseum, with thirty three different companies performing throughout the decade, the last ending in 1985.

At the end of the show, came the reverence, the company bow with the female dancers curtseying to the audience and the males bowing. The audience applauded with vigour before the final curtain calls, the opportunity for the individual lead dancers to also take their bows.

Rudolf Nureyev took his and the audience gave a standing ovation, underlined by sincere cheering. The whole theatre shook with the vibration from the applause the company received. But it all ended far too quickly for Julie and after Nureyev had disappeared from the Coliseum for the last time that night, silence once again prevailed.

She left the changing room with her ballet bag slung over one shoulder and eventually left the theatre through the stage door. As she did so, her mother was there to greet her with the biggest bouquet of flowers she had ever seen, filled with scented yellow roses, but the smile on her mother's face and the tears of pride in her eyes, were more precious to Julie than all the colour and greenery at the Chelsea Flower Show. Arm in arm, both mother and daughter caught the tube and made for home. Job done.

It was like continuing after the Lord Mayor's Show when Julie returned back to Rambert, but training went on as usual, as if nothing had happened. There was no room for doubt as far as Julie was concerned, she had made it, believing with all of her heart, a job was in the offering from the London Festival Ballet, so much so, she didn't bother circulating her photographs and curriculum vita to other companies. Perhaps foolish and arrogant at the time, but also understandable.

When the news finally came, which would be a deciding factor on her future career, Angela Ellis explained how Dame Beryl Gray had told her how pleased she had been with the girls dancing, behaviour and professional approach. Both students were overjoyed. Julie now had a one way ticket to success and everything else she had ever dreamed of. She never missed reaching that incredible benchmark of thirty two fouettes a day. At night she lay in bed, dreaming of bouquets of roses at the Royal Opera House in Covent Garden, the Bolshoi Theatre in Moscow, La Scala in Milan, the Sydney Opera House and the

Metropolitan Opera House in New York. The world was about to witness the birth of another Prima Ballerina. She knew that ballet companies are given the opportunity to offer contracts to the schools and that Rambert would have given that same opportunity to the London Festival Ballet. Oh how really, really wonderful life could be.

Then the day came when Angela Ellis approached her two girls that had impressed so much during the Nureyev Gala Performance, but the usual glint in her eyes was missing. She spoke directly to Julie and re-iterated what she had been told by Dame Beryl Gray.

"I'm afraid she believes there isn't anyway she could have a black girl in the corps de ballet Julie. I am so sorry, she believes that if they are white swans, they all have to be white swans and a black one would mess up the line."

"But if we had done such a good job, why hasn't she offered a contract to Mary?" asked Julie.

Mrs. Ellis had no answer to that and just shrugged her shoulders before leaving both girls to wallow in their misery.

Julie was devastated. Once again, her dreams had been shattered, only because of the colour of her skin. It wasn't right, it wasn't fair, how in God's name should anyone on this earth be punished because of the colour of their skin? She wanted to fight back, seek revenge for all the class snobbery that existed in the world and was preventing her from living her dream, but deep down she knew that wasn't the way, there was nothing that could be done against a foe that had existed since the beginning of civilisation. But she'd be damned if she was just going to roll over and keep accepting such racial insults as the one dispatched like a dagger to her heart by someone who she thought should have known better, Beryl Gray, bloody Dame Beryl Gray.

She stepped out from the building and stared up at the blackened sky above, which seemed to be responding to her mood by spitting out flashes of lightning. The rain came with the kind of vengeance lodged in Julie's heart, but still she just stood there, staring upwards, feeling God's wrath washing her face. She bit her lower lip and the rain hid the tears falling down her face. Why was life so cruel? Why were people with power in their hands so narrow minded? Why had she again, been left to feel like a poor wretch destined to live the rest of her days in life's basement, with only an old green couch to rest upon? No, she had strength, resolve, talent, artistic talent at that, and by God, the bastards were going to pay in the only way she knew how. Dig deep girl, back to that inner soul which was a maelstrom of unleashed genius, and prove to the world, a black girl could make it to the very top, no matter what the cost in human endeavour.

So, it would be back to the drawing board, no white flag, no surrender, continuing with even greater determination, with some help of course from that old green couch that now seemed to be calling to her to press on regardless. Be damned Dame Beryl Gray and damnation to the rest of the ballet fraternity. Let them all just watch this space. Brothers and sisters, once more Julie is back and raring to kick off once again.

She was only three months away from graduation and needed every second, every minute that was left to her to climb back up that mountain, from which she had so abruptly descended. Her friend and inspiration, Mary, was also despondent. The girls had never discussed the failure they had felt when subjected to such a heavy defeat, yet Julie felt as much sympathy for her closest ally as she did for herself. Then she received a phone call. Her old chum, Brenda, was back in town. So was the Dance Theatre Harlem.

According to Brenda, Harlem were about to start a two week season at Sadler's Wells, appearing at the Angel Theatre in Islington. As the possibility of another invitation for a company class reached her ears down the telephone line, the anger and frustration began to dissolve. This time there would be no hesitation, certainly no rejection. This time she told Angela Ellis and received her best wishes to do well, before heading for the theatre, in which one more opportunity awaited the black girl from Ealing.

As on the previous occasion, she quickly commenced her warming up exercises and was busy stretching her limbs when Arthur Mitchell appeared.

"So, you're back then?" he said with a wry smile on his handsome face.

"Yes."

The company founder and director laughed aloud and beckoned her to start her routine, which she did. After a couple of movements the verbal challenges to her character began to flow from Mitchell, hitting her like skimmers across a lake.

"What do you think you're doing English girl, your legs are too low, not turning out enough," and so on. The criticisms never seemed to stop throughout her dance executions, but this was the new sustained Julie and she knew he was testing her, expecting her to evaporate beneath his throw away insults. Each time he spoke in the negative, Julie gave some more, she won every battle by showing Arthur Mitchell she did have what it takes and some more. This was a donkey ride at the seaside compared with what she'd been through. If only her father had been there to witness first-hand the level of resolve his youngest daughter possessed. The fire in those black eyes, thanks to Dame Beryl Gray, hadn't left her, adding pulsating drama to the dancer's story, leaving other members of the company watching, flabbergasted and teased into the desire to see more.

The class finally came to an end and applause filled the studio. Julie never heard anything except her own frantic breathing, having given her all to that one performance, that one class. Neither did she overhear some of the comments that came from the rest of the guys and girls present.

"Boy, was that really something."

"That girl just ain't real, brother."

"I thought I'd seen it all in this business, I hadn't 'til now, feller."

After she had returned to the land of the living, Julie glanced up and found Arthur Mitchell's eyes. He was standing there like a statuette, staring down into that feminine facial carving. He spoke in a serious voice, "You've got a lot to learn girl..."

"Don't you go asking me to teach her boss," a voice called out from the floor, sparking off a small round of laughter.

"...I never offer a contract twice to anybody and I'm not forgetting I offered one to you last year at the Palladium and you turned your back on me, girl." He paused to allow time for the words of his statement to sink in and hopefully cool off some of the excitement that had filled the room. He still had to show he was the main man.

Not diverting his eyes from Julie's, he took a moment to observe, discover and analyse whatever was going on in this girl's head. Could he see disappointment, perhaps even distress? Well, the disappointment was there, but distress? Not in this girl, not in our Julie who no longer felt pain or fear. As far as she was concerned he was staring into the eyes of the greatest ballerina in the whole wide world.

"Any roads," he continued, lowering his voice, "I'm going to make an exception in your case, but if you turn this one down, don't bother coming back." Had Arthur Mitchell succeeded in maintaining his status as the man in charge. Sure he had, but only just.

Oh my Lord, thank you, thank you Lord, Julie Felix was going to become a professional dancer. Julie Felix, the little black girl from Ealing, London, England, was going to display her dancing talents to the world, in the States, Russia, Europe and any place else to where this wonderful man decided to take his company, of which she was about to become a member. Thank you again, Lord.

Her eyes lit up like fireworks night on November the Fifth. They sparkled like two black diamonds caught in the surf.

"Thank you, sir," she whispered, before lowering those excited eyes to the floor.

He nodded and mumbled something incoherent before turning to walk away.

"I love you, Mister Mitchell," she spontaneously said under her breath, not wanting her words to reach his ears.

Mitchell stopped abruptly and turned to face her.

Oh my God, how the hell did he hear that, she asked herself, feeling her heartbeat take off.

"Oh, and don't forget to see the company manager on the way out, girl."

Chapter Twelve

The Old Green Couch

Exciting and thrilling thoughts were now keeping Julie Felix's mind occupied. Taking over all logic and mental reasoning, pushing out her old friends, courage, commitment and self-motivation to someplace else. For a girl who had never really enjoyed roller coasters, limiting that particular adventurous activity to the creaking roundabout in her local Lammas Park, what she experienced during those few weeks following her success at the Angel Theatre in Islington, would have surpassed any thrill gained from any fairground ride.

She became dizzy with the various factions opposing each other, using her thoughts as their battalions and her mind as their battle field, convincing positive persuasions representing the goodies, opposed by those old adversaries, doubt and fear. But this was what she had devoted her life towards. This was what her parents had worked so hard for, to see their daughter happy and that was the key. No matter how much she jostled with the ins and outs of what lay in store for her, she was happy, even though happiness sometimes demands sacrifice. So, what sacrifices would be laid on the table of hope? She must leave home; leave her loved ones behind as she travelled the world. What would her boyfriend, Kevin, think about all of this? Rambert was shortly to be shed, after she had graduated, but that didn't make matters any easier.

Okay, so all the dancers in her new company were black. Who gave a damn, they were all ballet dancers and they would all be working, living together in America, revelling in the Big Apple. She would have to get a decent camera to click away at those towering skyscrapers and bright lights that made up the New York skyline.

She awoke each morning, not believing this was happening to her. It must all be a dream, a projected symptom of some viral infection she'd come down with, resulting in hallucinations of the most vivid kind. But, her future was clearly marked and her objectives remained the same as before, in that she was well on her way to proving the doubters wrong. She would spend twelve months with Harlem, earning the kind of reputation reserved only for Prima Ballerinas and then return to England, where she would stick up two fingers to those who had so cruelly rejected her and say out aloud, "Eh, you people, here I am, just come and get me."

Yes, sir, she would be proud and elegant, as she skipped and flew across the biggest stages in the world as a member of the Dance Theatre Harlem. She would be proud, she felt proud, she was going to mesmerise the world of ballet, with some help of course from that darling man, Arthur Mitchell.

Julie had never vacated English soil, she'd never flown before in her life and the call from Mitchell was to make New York as soon as possible, all expenses paid eventually, of course. She had to get a visa, graduate from Rambert, say goodbye to Kevin, who was seriously thinking over the possibility of joining up with her in the States, once he'd saved sufficient pennies for his airfare. That could prove more difficult than he'd let on, as the bloke had never had a job and didn't seem the type to ever get one, except perhaps as the skipper of a shark boat.

She was consoled by the fact her contract was for twelve months, although that would also mean that in a year's time she would be back in Britain, registering as an unemployed person, perhaps. Angela Ellis had tried to explain that it was far better to have a job before finishing at Rambert, than having to leave the school without any prospect of work and of course, the lady was absolutely right. There were already too many out of work dancers roaming the streets, looking for anything that would help to pay for the next meal, and she didn't really fancy joining that particular queue.

As for her parents, well, her mother was obviously overjoyed but the real surprise came when Julie learned that her father, Patrick, had been flaunting himself around the neighbourhood of Ealing, boasting that his youngest daughter was off to the Big Apple to become a star. He had always dreamed of placing his feet on American soil, as a young man he, like so many others, had been seriously influenced by the Hollywood film industry and all that had been portrayed of the States. But now, his daughter would be giving him a connection to his dream, a bridge of immense pride upon which he would never cross, but would be content to know a part of him had crossed the Atlantic and made home over there.

So, all in all, Julie had support from all the loved ones in her life, which would be invaluable to her when her mind drifted to thoughts of New York City and what the Metropolis was really like. One thing she wouldn't be doing was returning home in disgrace. There was no way she was going to let anyone down, quite the contrary, the girl was hell bent on achieving beyond anybody's expectations, including her own. This wasn't Nureyev, who had defected from Russia, leaving his own country of birth behind in his wake; this particular dancer would remain proud of her heritage and strive to make everyone else aware of just that. Therefore, with the same courage and endeavour only a young ambitious and extremely talented young lady could muster, all disturbing thought patterns about her future were bombed out and the process of leaving her home and moving to the USA got under way.

She listened out of courtesy to all the reassurance everyone was giving her, explaining that this was to be an amazing experience, a tremendous learning curve as a ballet dancer and as a person.

Thankfully, her mother was her tower of strength, remaining cool, calm and collected in every sense and situation, often sparking Julie's memories of those times when she would sit, watching her mother preparing for an operatic performance. The make-up being applied with a steady hand and the usual question, "Mum, don't you feel nervous?" The answer was always the same, "If you breathe correctly and stay mindful and focused, nervousness never affected your performance." Julie loved her mother dearly for the things she taught her as a young girl, lessons that would never been forgotten.

She continued working at McDonald's, until she'd saved up enough money to pay for her flight, determined to take away some of the financial stress off her parents. Then the day finally arrived, the day which would be her last at Rambert, the day she would graduate and leave the school behind her.

As the train descended into the darkness of an underground tunnel, she caught the reflection of herself in the window. There sat a young lady staring back, but who was this woman she asked herself, remembering the young teenager who used to travel on the same route and who had developed into an adult female so quickly. 'I am who I am,' her reflection answered back. But there was no more time for consultation, as the train stopped and she stepped off for the last time.

It was strange how everything looked different, the people, the cars and even the blue cloudless sky. Everything appeared unreal, as if she had been transported to another time. Of course, she was susceptible to mind games at that particular moment in her life, but who wouldn't have been considering the minefield she'd managed to overcome.

The day slowly dragged by, seeming to last forever and as the dusk began to fall on Nottinghill Gate, the moment came to actually say her final farewells. Personal contact numbers and home addresses were exchanged together with hugs and kisses. Tears rolled down young faces and handshakes were warm, expressions sorrowful, including those who had supported all the students from their hideaway in the school office. Julie even stopped on the narrow landing and touched the pane of glass with genuine tenderness, the same one through which Jane had fallen through, so long ago. She deliberately left the basement until last, the sanctuary, the monumental shrine to all that had gone on before.

She stood motionless in the doorway with her eyes closed, taking in for the final time, the atmosphere and smell of that wonderful small room. She stepped down the stairs into the room itself and allowed her memories to come flooding back, remembering the gasps of pain, the blaspheming, laughter and anger she and Mary shared during their years trying hard to climb up the ladder of achievement. It was difficult, how so difficult to turn her eyes towards that old green couch, but it beckoned to her once again and she obliged by stepping across the room, before running her long slim fingers along the top of the back rest.

"Thank you so much for everything," she quietly whispered, paying homage to the ancient piece of furniture that had witnessed all the anguish and suffering the girls had put themselves through. All the years of rejection, all met with courage and determination that had led her to this point in her life when she had grasped the crown of achievement.

She had no idea how long she stayed, rubbing her face and tears against that old couch, but couldn't leave without feeling Mary's supporting hand resting on her shoulder. Hearing her own voice whisper, "Thank you, Mary, let's go and get a hot chocolate. Thank you again green couch and thank you Rambert for all you have done for me. You will all remain in my heart forever, I promise."

'Farewell, a long farewell, to all my greatness! This is the state of man; today he puts forth the tender leaves of hope; tomorrow blossoms.' William Shakespeare.

Julie believed her tears of farewell represented the depth of feeling she had for others and the experiences they had shared, a reservoir of memories which could be siphoned off if ever needed in the future. Perhaps they were all aimed towards those experiences of life that melt when sadness looms.

She couldn't leave Rambert on that final day without saying farewell to Angela Ellis. She searched in earnest to find the lady to whom she owed so much, asking in the school office, enquiring with other students and teachers, but no one had seen her. Similar to a lost child looking for its mother in a crowded supermarket, she ran to the upper tier, back down again, then the lady appeared, slowly walking towards her, with eyes filled with a mixture of pleasure, pride and sadness.

Had Julie been one of Mrs. Ellis's 'special students'? Had she really been different from all those other dancers who had walked through the doors and graced the floors of the dance studios at Rambert Ballet School? One thing she did know was that she felt honoured to have been a significant part of the institution's history.

Angela Ellis opened her arms and her student fell into them, embracing each other, held in a brief time warp, exchanging the kind of chemistry from which love, pride and adoration manifested. Julie was a success, the lady teacher had done her job well, but it was now all over. Standing back a step she stared into Julie's tearful eyes and spoke softly, "Well done, my little bird of freedom. Remember all that I have taught you. Be brilliant darling and never forget your roots and where you came from. Be brave and never lack the courage you have shown to me throughout your stay with us."

They would never meet again in person and Julie clung on for a little longer, not wanting this particular lady who had been an icon to her, to disappear forever, desperate to absorb the last few drops of this amazing woman's influence. Then Angela Ellis let go and turned, before drifting away, back to the normality of her own life, leaving her student alone, still sobbing like a helpless baby. It was also time for Julie to depart and once outside, she stood for a moment, taking in one last final look at what had been her home during the most important years of her life, remembering that small, immature black girl who had first entered through those double doors, full of so much anxiety and apprehension. That little black girl who had so much to learn and still had, according to her new mentor, Arthur Mitchell. Of course she knew she could never turn the clock back, she would never return to those tortuous but wonderful days, but vowed to herself and to Rambert that she would always strive to improve and continue in her new ambition, which

was to always come home.

Chapter Thirteen

The Long Farewell

The Royal Mail must have increased their business two fold after Julie discovered the costly service known as air mail. The number of communications that swept to and fro across the Atlantic, between Dance Theatre Harlem and Patrick Felix's house must have excelled the daily traffic between Downing Street and the White House. DTH requested Julie's passport details and a reply was sent confirming their new recruit's passport had not yet arrived. Then came the next airmail letter from DTH asking reasons for the delay? Perhaps it was because the Customs and Excise Department had discovered Julie was in fact an escaped Lifer from some Category A prison, or was the subject of some spy scandal up in the Midlands. Such an explanation was tempting, but she resisted. Whatever the true reason, each time Julie paid for the cost of sending an air mail reply, another came back asking more questions, including a demand that she made it to New York as soon as possible, as her presence was urgently required.

The air mail saga continued until Julie's mother came up with a positive idea. "Julie, why don't we get ourselves a telephone?" The suggestion was heaven sent. How on earth had the Felix family, like the majority of households in the country, ever coped without a telephone, bearing in mind that some twenty years later, every kid in the street would have one attached to their ear. So, thanks to good old mum, a telephone was ordered and quickly installed by a couple of Post Office engineers. It wasn't as easy as all that though, they'd forgotten to discuss the matter over with Patrick, well at least until after Alexander Bell's invention had been fitted and wired up. Then one day and after a few transatlantic calls had already been made, Julie overheard a conversation between her mother and father.

"Julie is costing us so much money with this dancing business. At least Lucia is standing on her own two feet. She hasn't asked us for anything. How do we know if Julie will make it in New York? How do we know if she will make it at all with this dancing of hers? Now you tell me you've spent more money on getting this telephone for her."

"Perhaps one day, Patrick, you might want to make a call to America or even Saint Lucia," her mother answered back.

That seemed to give her husband a different angle to his way of thinking and the subject was never again approached. Well done, Doreen.

Feeling just a little guilty, their youngest daughter sympathised with her father's views, so promised to send her first pay cheque from Harlem back home to help pay for that bloody new telephone. Very soon afterwards, what three air mail letters would have contained, was spoken at first hand over the transatlantic lines in just short of a minute. Thank you Mr. Alexander Bell.

Time raced by and the long awaited visa and passport finally arrived safely. A suitcase was packed and close friends said their final farewells, including Mary of the old green couch fame, who also left Julie with her address. By then the tears had dried up and it was just a case of dealing with a trembling lower lip, but New York was calling, loud and clear. Julie's heartbeat was in overdrive and her mind becoming more like a spectacular sky filled with transparent bags of stardust.

Her boyfriend Kevin, didn't want to say his goodbye at the airport, but instead promised to join up with her in New York, in about three months' time, after the shark fishing season had ended. So, the wait finally came to an end, the day had arrived, the transatlantic flight was waiting on the airport apron with its jet engines warming up and its hospitality staff waiting in readiness to greet the future Ballerina.

The taxi arrived on time, having had no problem finding the brightly coloured front door. Patrick Felix, dressed as immaculately as ever in a double breasted suit, Humphrey Bogart style trilby and two- tone shoes, led the way across the pavement, no doubt inviting those watching the small cavalcade leave, wondering which of the Felix family was actually leaving for the States. He was followed by Mum, who looked adorable in her Sunday best dress, coat and hat, with Julie last but not least.

As they were transported across London to Heathrow, emotions were running high. For most of the journey, all three sat in the back of the taxi in utter silence. For Julie's part, she felt as if she had the weight of the whole world on her shoulders, ready to release a cascading torrent of tears and trying hard to strengthen the dam holding them back. She was about to fly out alone, all the way to America, with no one to speak to, not knowing anybody well enough to speak to. How the bloody hell had she thought herself capable of ever undertaking such a nightmare trip as the one she was about to undertake? Why in God's name could she not have been offered a job in England? After all, that had been the plan, hadn't it? Why all this, having to travel halfway across the world just to progress her career? Had it been her selfishness that had brought this day on? It all seemed so unfair now. Stop the taxi cabbie and turn it around. I want to go home, please, oh please.

The traffic signs for Heathrow began to loom in the distance and Julie began to feel cold, feverish even. She was beginning the early symptoms of homesickness before her feet had even left the ground. Then the taxi stopped, right outside the terminal and her father got out to pay the cabbie. Doreen's eyes rested on her daughter's; she was going to cry there and then, they were both going to cry there and then. No, they mustn't, they still had to get inside the airport building, but that didn't stop time from freezing for a fleeting moment.

Unknown to each other, a lifetime of memories flashed before them. Julie was being cradled in her mother's arms as a helpless baby, blowing bubbles in the air. Then she was standing, hiding behind her mother's apron whenever someone knocked on Patrick's now famous front door.

"If you wasn't so thin and ate all of your dinners, that would never have happened." Remembering those words caused her mother to smile, as the memory of her young daughter came back to her, wringing wet and freezing cold, having just visited the duck pond.

'Please don't cry oh mother of mine; how dear you have been. My closest friend and confidante. My oath and my love, you have always been there for me; you have never let me down. Please don't cry.'

It was time to leave her, Julie's dearest mum, and the pain was unimaginable. She felt her heart being torn from her chest and this kind of hellish trauma would never be forgotten or repeated. Then, reality was resumed by the sound of her father's voice yelling for both of his ladies to hurry up and get out of the taxi, before Julie missed her flight. God bless Patrick Felix for his practicalities.

Patrick took hold of his daughter's suitcase and dragged it to the check-in desk, while Doreen took one final opportunity to quickly run over those small things she needed her daughter to be certain about, including those matters of the utmost importance that only adult women should know about.

Passport produced for examination, boarding pass issued and handed over, suitcase accepted and driven to the hold. It was done and all that was left now was for Julie to disappear air side and await the call up of her flight number. They exchanged for one last time, hugs and kisses. Now it was time for the tears to flow rivers and the pain in Patrick's eyes confirmed his absolute feeling of loss. Julie then turned abruptly, in similar fashion to how Angela Ellis had left her back at Rambert, and disappeared from her parents' sight. Their little girl was leaving them to begin a new adventure, three thousand miles away, an adventure that they had all worked until they had nigh on dropped, to facilitate. Doreen Felix must have been wondering what her beautiful ballet star would be like when she next set eyes on her. Would she be the straight standing, proud and accomplished woman of the world, she hoped she would be? Time would tell, in fact, the following twelve months would provide that answer.

Julie walked tall and straight, down a corridor leading to Passport Control, her eyes wet and feeling like a prisoner walking to the gas chamber. She looked straight ahead, refusing to turn around where only grief was stalking her. But thank you Mother, thank you Father, for giving me life and this talent I possess.

As the Aer Lingus plane left the ground, bound for John F Kennedy Airport, there was England, below her, at her feet, with its green meadows interspersed by a network of lanes and roads, moving dots and shades of colour, the sight of which could only be reserved for those of us flying so high, so free.

Part Three
Dance Theatre Harlem

Chapter Fourteen

Welcome to America

Three thousand miles across the Atlantic Ocean at thirty six thousand feet wasn't bad for a maiden flight and Julie sat back, gazing out of a window, frightened, anxious, trying hard not to worry about the plane suddenly turning over or somersaulting down the runway. She had unwittingly gasped as the engines roared and the plane dramatically accelerated, before leaving the ground. She was terrified as the flight gained more height, leaving the dark clouds behind and soaring up into that vast sea of dazzling blue with the Earth's curvature on the horizon

When her scrambled thoughts finally returned to some kind of normality, she wondered what New York was really like. Was there more to the city than gangsters, film stars, murders, robberies, hamburgers and popcorn? The teenage girl was soon to find out.

Her first step on American soil was at John F Kennedy Airport and Julie's first stop was at Passport Control where she was interrogated at length by Immigration Officers carrying holstered guns, which added to the strange alien feeling now beginning to take hold.

In some of those many airmail communications from the Dance

Theatre Harlem she'd been warned about the legalities and restrictions American Immigration placed on visitors to the States. So, she had to get her story straight and when asked, declared that she was only visiting for three months to study and not to work. She couldn't show her twelve month working contract and almost freaked out under the barrage of questions put to her.

"How long do you intend to stay?"

"Why have you come to America?"

"Are you sure you're here to study and not work?"

"What do you mean, you're undertaking an apprenticeship here? Lady, that's the same as being employed in our book, so again, how long do you intend to stay here?"

"Where's your return ticket?"

Then her imagination began to kick in.

"Sorry, lady, but we can't let you in, Miss Fatty here, the one with the bazooka across her shoulder will take you into custody, where you will be kept in one of our cells until we can get you a flight back to where you've come from."

"You mean to say, I'm being deported?"

"No, ma'am, you're being arrested and will have to face charges relating to your fraudulent claims made to unlawfully enter our country once we've kicked your arse out of here."

But the girl from England forged on, eventually managing to persuade her inquisitors she really was visiting their country to study ballet and nothing more, even if she still felt the urge to tell the world she was going to be a famous ballerina.

After muddling her way through Immigration, she at least managed to retrieve her luggage, pushing her suitcase on a trolley through masses of people who all seemed to be chattering, busily going nowhere in particular, like lost ants looking for their nest. When she had the audacity to ask for help or directions, she was either rebuffed or met with blank faces, shocked by the sight of this girl with what might have been a thick beard down to her navel, or a wired aerial sticking out of her head.

"Go ask a cop, lady," or "Go take a hike, black girl," or, she was just completely ignored. Julie's first impression of all Americans was that they were rude, arrogant and racist. Oh how she longed to be back with her parents and in the comfort and safety of her own bedroom back home.

At least her pre-travel research had left her with some knowledge of this vast arena of diversity. For instance, she had been told never to take a taxi in New York unless it was a yellow cab. Pirates lurked on every street corner, willing to pick up a naïve tourist or visitor who was totally ignorant of the American way of life, people who would take you to your required destination, only to charge the earth for getting you there. And if you refused to pay extortionate prices, you were taken miles from where you wanted to go and unceremoniously dumped. So, that was her first task as a free person having successfully gained entry into the United States, join the lengthy queue that waited for a yellow cab.

Her cabbie was an elderly gentleman dressed in an Hawaiian style heavy flowered cotton sleeveless shirt, with grey hair and a friendly smile. She seemed to recognise this particular advert for potting plants and flowering shrubs, who reminded her uncannily of the same gent who'd spoke to her during her audition for *Mother Goose*, but no, it couldn't have been. His voice sounded the same but his broad accent was obviously local to New York. She wondered if he had a brother back in England.

"Could you take me please to the Webster Home for Girls on 34th Street at 8th Avenue?" she asked, reading from a list of directions, provided by the ballet company.

"Sure, miss, we're on our way. My name's Sam, what are you doing here in New York?"

"I'm Julie," she replied, "I'm here to perform ballet with the Dance Theatre Harlem."

"Eh, that sounds great, a real life ballerina eh? Well, you might be having a hard time at the moment, Julie, but don't let that worry you none, once you get used to us yanks, you'll enjoy it over here." Yes, he certainly sounded a lot like the *Mother Goose* man, even though he spoke through a partially open bullet proof glass partitioning that divided the front from the back of the cab. At least she felt at ease, talking to someone at last about why she had travelled all the way from London and what she was there for. In fact she became pre-occupied chatting away with the talkative and friendly old man with the tropical flower arrangement on his shirt, until they approached one of the bridges that would take them from the mainland to Manhattan. It was then she was suddenly taken aback by the Manhattan skyline with the two World Trade Centres, the Statue of Liberty and Empire State Building, all magnificently reaching up to the sky and breath taking.

"So Julie, what do you think of our scenery?" the cabbie, Sam asked.

"It's unbelievable."

She saw a smile on his face in the driver's rear view mirror which meant he was obviously pleased with her reply. In fact Sam would have also been pleased with the way his fare had changed from a nervous, lonely and cautious girl, to one who was showing a lot more spirit and confidence now.

They finally reached 34th Street at 8th Avenue and the yellow cab stopped right outside a large red brick building, which resembled an office block and was situated close to the famous Macy's Store. The Webster Home for Girls, recommended to her by the DTH reminded Julie of a YWCA at home, which she later found was just as basic in accommodation.

She offered Sam the same amount of cash in dollars as was displayed on his meter and he immediately responded by telling her he'd enjoyed her company that much, she only had to pay half the fare. He got a courteous 'thank you' and gleaming smile in return. The problem Julie then had was leaving the taxi. She was so reluctant to leave the comfort and safety of that cab, but did so only after the old man had told her, "Lady, there's a lot of bad places in this town, but this ain't one of them. You'll be okay, just trust old Sam here."

As she approached the front doors, she hesitated and scanned her eyes over the building, realising this was to be her home for the next year or so. Would she hold it together? You could bet your bottom American dollar she would.

The place reminded her a little of Rambert, with a small office located just inside the front entrance and a tall, elderly black man, standing almost at attention, to greet newcomers. He was dressed in the kind of battered peaked flat hat which looked as though it had spent most of its life under the wheel of a tramcar. The rest of his shabby uniform was also a perfect match with his head gear. But he appeared friendly enough and commented on how far away from home she was, adding, "We'll take good care of you here, miss," after she'd introduced herself.

Julie was given the key to room number 1006 on the tenth floor and quickly began the last part of her long journey by using a small lift which held up to three people maximum, that was if they had all been on a strict diet. She reached the tenth floor and carried her suitcase down a long, dark corridor, with rooms either side. Finally she arrived at her new habitation, opened the door and stepped inside. Yep, she got it right when comparing the place with a YWCA. In fact it could have been a nun's room in a convent, with its single bed, wash basin, cupboard, desk and one chair; it was that basic. There was a bathroom down the corridor outside and she soon discovered there was communal eating, calls being made over a communications system that used to blast out to announce when the next meal was ready to be served.

Surprisingly, she read on a small 'dos and don'ts' list on one of the walls, which were all painted in a sort of mid green colour, that the doors to the establishment were locked at 10.30 p.m. sharp and not re-opened until 6.0 a.m. the following morning. So, here she was, incarcerated in this residence for girls, having to live without the comforts of home or the support of friends and family. She could only hope that during the winter months, the heating was switched on. Having dropped her suitcase on the floor, Julie just sat on the bed and cried her eyes out.

Chapter Fifteen

Harlem

The following day began with Julie facing her first hurdle, somehow making Harlem without being accosted or robbed, or even worse. The mental picture she carried with her was the main cause of her anxiety, compiled from what she'd heard and read about the notorious black community's main district, which always sent a shudder up her spine.

After making some initial enquiries about how the hell she got there and resisting the temptation to purchase a suit of armour, her plan of travel was simple, or so she thought. Firstly, she would have to ride the Manhattan subway to 145th Street and then walk the rest of the way to where DTH was located, right in the middle of Harlem. Old Sam the cabbie had assured her the district in which the home for lost girls was located, was safe enough, but he hadn't mentioned anything about Harlem.

For a lonely girl, all the way from the other side of the Atlantic, it wasn't an ordeal she'd been looking forward to, but she just had to make it, so with shoulders pressed back, head held high, teeth gritted together and her ballet bag over one shoulder, she strode away from the Webster House in search of glory.

At least people seemed to be more approachable during the early morning hustle and bustle, which was surprising after what she'd experienced the day before, even one or two gents raised their hats in greeting to her. Following instructions, she managed to purchase a token to ride the subway, quickly boarding her train and sitting near a window, keeping a tight grip on her ballet bag, which contained everything she owned in the world. Her guard was constantly up and her eyes never failed to watch and observe everything and everybody around her. Then she noticed a young black kid standing in the middle aisle, staring at her. She thought about that time back in London when a flasher decided to attract her attention, and wondered whether the same was about to happen again. Surprisingly, there weren't that many other people in the carriage, so she continued to stare out of the window, trying hard to pretend she was interested in the contrasting architecture of some of the tallest high risers in the world.

Another girl was sitting just in front of Julie, so she decided to speak to her, if only to convince any interested party, she wasn't travelling alone.

"Excuse me, but is this the right train for Harlem?"

But the girl just nodded without speaking and turned her attention to something invisible on her lap.

"Eh, sister," the black kid finally called out, moving towards Julie. He looked as though he was in desperate need of a square meal and was dressed only in a dirty white tee shirt and grey jeans, "Where you from, sister?" he asked.

Julie was petrified, wondering whether this black hobo was going to pull a knife on her, or perhaps even a gun. At first she stuttered, but managed to speak, rather courageously if it come to that, "I'm not your sister and I'm from London, England. My father's a well-known policeman over there." She had no idea why she had said that, later recalling that if she intended to scare the kid off, that would have gone down like a lead balloon.

But the intruder, who paused with a gaping mouth, obviously taken aback by the girl's no nonsense response, said nothing more because the train suddenly stopped at Julie's 145th Street. She left her seat and made for the nearest open door like a Giselle, hoping and praying the guy didn't follow her. Fortunately, he didn't, but that didn't help her feel less than scared out of her wits, all the way to 152nd Street. She did notice as she briskly walked, a woman sitting in the middle of the street urinating, but this was Harlem and she had to just accept whatever was served up.

Opening her eyes wider, she looked around and saw what Harlem in those days was really about. Poor souls lying in the streets, saturated in wine and whatever other rot gut spirits they'd consumed, junkies shouting out like demented patients on a day release from an asylum somewhere, piles of garbage on street corners, and kids drinking from water hydrants that were leaking. There was dirt and filth just about everywhere. This was a far cry from Ealing or Notting Hill.

She walked past a basketball square surrounded by a high wire fence with a bunch of black kids playing ball, seemingly oblivious to all that was going on around them. This was their world in the same way as Julie's was a studio floor where she lived through her fantasies by dancing; that patch of ground belonged to those kids, it was their sanctuary and safety net which kept them sane and almost respectable. In fact, Julie had never seen so many black people before in her life, having had no black friends back in London. This was all very new to her and very frightening. What she didn't realise at the time was that Julie was seeing everything through white eyes, having thought, lived and breathed in the same way as the white English people with whom she had been raised.

Finally, she made it to her destination and stood just inside the front door with worried eyes scanning a hallway, which had a set of wide steps going up to the first landing. All the walls were made of exposed brickwork and most of them were covered with Dance Theatre Harlem posters and enlarged copies of programs from various performances. There were ballet mirrors and barres everywhere and very soon a dancer who immediately recognised her from London, approached and welcomed Julie like a long lost sister. She soon settled and was quickly taken to the changing rooms, being introduced to every person she met or passed by. Welcome to Harlem Julie.

Her first day at DTH was mostly all about meeting the gang and doing a few warm up exercises, chatting about the next performance and in particular the kind of man Arthur Mitchell was, who didn't show up on that occasion. When the day's end finally came, she changed and made her way back on foot to the subway, passing the same basketball patch, which she thought was still occupied by the same kids she'd seen that morning. But the only thing on her mind as she made 145th Street, was the events of the day and she was excited, having really enjoyed that first introduction to life away from Rambert. Perhaps, once she learned to push her thoughts of home to the back of her mind, things might not be so bad, here in this strange world of good guys and bad guys, riches and poverty. Then her optimistic thoughts were dramatically interrupted by loud shouts, coming from the opposite sidewalk.

"Hit the ground, sister," one feller shouted from somewhere nearby, so she did without hesitation, crouching in the dust, grasping her ballet bag more tightly and wondering what the hell was going to happen next. Then she saw him, the same black kid who had approached her on the subway, earlier that morning. The lad was running hell for leather from a store he'd obviously just robbed, with what looked like two plain clothes cops close on his trail. They had the widest girths she'd ever seen and were both wearing large black leather belts around their waists that held more different types of weapons Julie could expect to see in a lifetime.

People seemed to disappear off the streets, as if they'd just heard over the wires that aliens from another world were about to land and obliterate New York. It was obvious the two fatties were never going to catch the younger, slimmer and more agile robber, so they called for him to stop as he approached a patch of open ground, threatening to fire if he declined their invitation. The kid just carried on sprinting away like Arkle winning the Derby.

So, both heavies dropped to one knee in exactly the same way those crime busters do in the movies, drew a bead on their target with their hand guns and opened up. The lad must have been hit by at least half a dozen .38 dum-dum bullets from both guns, interrupting the kid's flow and causing him to jerk left, then right, with both arms and legs grasping for something that wasn't there. He hit the ground spread eagled, covered in his own blood. A strange kind of stillness took over the whole street and the only sound was the echo of the cops walking towards their prey.

'Where you from, sister,' lay perfectly still, not moving a muscle and obviously as dead as the roll of banknotes grasped in one of his hands. How she wished Sam the cabbie was around at that precise moment.

She regained her feet, staring across at the dead kid, feeling a flood of sympathy for that same black lad, who she now realised had called her 'sister,' only because they both had the same colour skin. It was just the way in which black males addressed black females in America and the shame and pity she felt went deep, but there was nothing she could do, although she would never forget the look on that young black face when he asked an innocent question, like "Where you from, sister?" Yes, how she wished she had been at least more civil towards him, when he was alive and breathing.

It was a New York Police Commissioner, William Bratton who first introduced a policy of 'zero-tolerance' policing, much later during the 1990's when the city was doing its best to get rid of the dreadful crime image earned over the previous three decades. The basic principle behind Bill Bratton's strategy was to arrest individuals committing minor crime with a view to preventing their inevitable future major crimes. The policy succeeded and is well documented. Even after Bratton's tenure came to an end, Mayor Bloomberg continued with its success, fighting against opposing factions that claimed, although criminals were taken off the streets and cracking down on relatively minor offences helped to prevent future crime from being committed, the cost in money and man power to the city wasn't worth it. But at least it cleaned up Harlem and other down and out districts and the random shootings, knifings and killings were minimised.

Welcome to New York, Julie. In just twenty four hours of living in the Big Apple, she'd witnessed extreme poverty and everything that went with it, a killing of a young black kid and a woman pissing in the street without a care in the world. Yep, welcome to our city Julie.

Chapter Sixteen

Getting to Know You

Those first few weeks in New York were bewildering and at times confusing for Julie, feeling like a stranger lost in a maze and unable to find the main corridor down which everyone else stepped. It was more than a new life she had begun; it was as though she had been thrown into an entanglement of different cultures, social meanings, different ways and attitudes of a people that lived in a parallel universe to her own. And yet they lived their lives to the full, exaggerating most things and vociferously making their opinions known to everyone else.

Everything seemed to be based around segregation, whether it was the obvious separation of blacks from whites or living in a hostel, available only to females. Webster House was more than just an accommodation for women; it was their haven. Brief discussions over dinner helped her to understand more, quickly realising that some of her fellow lodgers had been the victims of bad relationships with men and were quite happy to continue in their bolt hole away from the male species.

Of course Harlem was Harlem and the dance company was an

extension of that district, with something to prove. Being amongst so many black people for the first time widened Julie's perspective on life and the daily necessity to prove that black people could dance ballet to perfection was like an infectious bug, which affected everyone in the company. But such a philosophy brought with it, higher expectation and harder and more aggressive work than she'd ever known before.

Arthur Mitchell, or Mr. Mitchell as he preferred to be called, was a harder task master than even Angela Ellis. Members of the company were grilled and made to practice daily, through the most gruelling pain and physical demands, with only one objective in mind; to mould their bodies into the black versions of white swans. It was as though the DTH was an outlet for dispelling all the anger and frustration provided by historical events involving the demise of black people in America over the centuries; an invisible safety valve.

She admired the other members' dedication and commitment for the Dance and appreciated the outstanding artistic talent she was rubbing shoulders with. But achievement and recognition were the key principles, both in the black communities and more importantly, in the white dominated field of The Ballet. Success at any cost? Most probably.

Julie's ballet master was a co-director of the company, Karl Shook, who frequently asked much of his dancers. Sixteen grande battemans, high kicks to the front, referred to as devant and to the side, la seconde and finally to the back, known as derriere, before returning to high kicks to the side. The women dancers would be required to pirouette at least triples constantly, where the men had to do the same movement for at least four or five rotations. The male dancers were never given any respite and their daily exercises involved double tour en lairs, jumping high into the air, turning twice before landing in a perfect fifth position. And all of that was always required before actual rehearsals began. This was indeed a much higher professional level she'd been used to and there was no hesitation from Julie as she threw herself wholeheartedly into the exercises.

This was indeed a different place for Julie, a place where professionalism and confidence excelled with each performer representing an individual element of a beautiful piece of well-oiled and polished machinery. Nothing less than nigh on perfection was acceptable and yet, there was always a splendid atmosphere, created by achievement and humour.

The company's repertoire varied considerably, favouring a composite of classical ballet and neo-classical ballet. In other words, a choreography or ethnic style of ballet coupled with a jazz theme, all put together by the Russian choreographer, George Balanchine, whose many achievements included being the co-founder of the New York City Ballet.

The kind of work Balanchine brought to the studio catapulted Julie into a new world of fascination, one in which she moved with ease, style and grace. But, to maintain the kind of level such enchantment required to meet its demands, life became harder and she often stayed behind after normal working hours to continue working by herself, missing dinner at Webster House. There were occasions when a friend, Nancy, who was also staying at the same hostelry, would manage to put a piece of bread, some ham and fruit on one side for when Julie finally returned to the lodgings. Of course, such abuse of her digestive system and body in general had its downside and Julie soon found herself topping just seven stone on the scales.

She had no problems during her working hours, training, practicing, rehearsing, they all managed to keep her mind focused. But away from the studio, she remained lonely and homesick. She rarely missed a night when she would sit on her bed and cry her eyes out, whispering her mother's name to herself. She wrote letters home with poems attached, hoping that would help ease the pain, but it never did. The black cloud that consumed her, only disappeared once she stepped through the doors of the studio and began her work in earnest.

As the weeks passed by, she at least managed to come to terms with life in general. For instance, riding on the subway didn't have the same frightening affect it once had. Being surrounded by strange looking minions who had the same colour skin as herself, became more natural and far less concerning. Eventually, Julie's adventurous spirit began to return until it finally broke through the depressing fog, opening a door through which the confident and audacious little black girl from Ealing, who had existed so long ago, returned.

She made friends, which included Nancy, another bubbling, full of life student at the Dance Theatre Harlem, who was also staying at the Webster House. She was from Poughkeepsie, in New York State and Julie liked the All American girl, pleased to have her as a train buddy when travelling to and from Harlem.

So, the two girls decided to explore, travelling to all points of the compass, whenever they were given the opportunity. A couple of pioneers, seeking the new world, or rather the world in which so many social variations and different cultures existed. The location where Webster House was situated and up to 42nd Street was known as mid-town. To the south of the city lies China Town, Little Italy and what became Julie's favourite place on her many tours, Greenwich Village. Her opinion of Greenwich was that it seemed quaint, similar to a picture postcard which also reminded her very much of England.

Up-town was where the gentry lived, the white dominated districts which boasted the Metropolitan Opera House and Lincoln Square, all so contrasting from the Harlem set up. Central Park is bang in the middle of the city and the two travelling young ladies found it to be respectable enough to visit during daylight hours. The only places in New York that

Julie had been warned against visiting was the Bronx and, of course, Harlem.

She was amazed by the volume of people who lived on such a small island as Manhattan, which in Julie's mind was nothing more than a melting pot, simmering but not boiling over as long as white authorities left Harlem well alone.

"Hey, sister, where you think you're going?"

"To work?" It seemed so strange how the word 'work' was always accompanied by a high shrill of piss taking disbelief.

"So where's this work you're going to, sister?"

"I work at the Dance Theatre Harlem, bruv."

Whichever black guy was asking the questions would then fold down on to the pavement, kicking his legs in the air and in rapturous laughter, notifying the rest of the population in Harlem that he'd just been on the receiving end of a joke.

"Go to it, ballet dancer lady."

Julie was quickly beginning to see the funny side of these impoverished people, feeling their unusual warmth and friendliness, which removed fear and concerns from her mind.

On one Sunday in particular, she and Nancy were walking down 5th Avenue, chatting away like a couple of Ginger Rogers, sharing snippets of information, when they were suddenly confronted by a magnificent church with two pointed steeples reaching for the sky, in all its glory. The century old building stood like some beckoning sentinel, a brilliant and illuminous white effigy, set against a cloudless blue sky. Julie had never before seen such a magnificent piece of awesome architecture as Saint Patrick's Cathedral, and stood for a moment, as if in communication with every carefully placed piece of neo-Gothic stone.

As she climbed the wide steps and entered through heavily carved wooden doors, leaving Nancy to continue the rest of their tour alone, the stillness inside hit her as if she was standing on some mountain top in the Swiss Alps, leaving Manhattan outside, together with its wailing sirens and honking horns. She stood for a brief moment in that peaceful silence, craning her neck to look up, overcome by the splendour of the magnificent high vaulted ceiling and impressive relief on stone columns and supports. Rows of polished wooden seats gave way to a narrow central aisle up which the girl from England walked slowly, towards the dominating altar.

She sat with her head bowed, her mind brimming with all kinds of stirring emotions, but completely at peace in this unexpected place of solitude. Julie had the opportunity to spread a little thanks to those who had helped her throughout her short life and to those who were still helping her to show off her wonderful talent to the rest of the world, so she prayed.

They say that prayers can come in various forms and Julie had no idea whether she was showing appreciation to God, her parents, or the Dance Theatre Harlem, but it mattered not. She was praying and in her prayers showing both gratitude and humility. Tears began to roll and land on her clasped hands. Self-control and internal discipline had disappeared for the time being, closing the door behind. It all came out, all the pent up feelings of complexity, all the shock resulting from the physical exertion she'd been subjected to, the needless worries and anxieties, like a volcano erupting and throwing all of the earth's garbage out through the top of her head.

"Tears can be good for the soul Julie," a soft, friendly voice whispered. It was Sam the cabbie, sitting somewhere behind her, "But, strength and desire will bring you success and get you home, trust me."

She looked up and with a broad smile, turned to greet him, but Sam wasn't there. Her eyes searched the empty pews, but there was no sign. Had she imagined that old man's voice? She would never know.

Chapter Seventeen

Mayhem in the Dark

Julie's quick learning ability had to eventually lead her down the road of comparisons and she soon discovered that, whereby the English looked towards achievement with an element of flexibility, her American colleagues had a more gung ho approach, in other words, go getters seemed a more appropriate description of their everyday overtures. The English were much more complacent, whereas it was fine to fall behind now and again and catch up later, but to the Americans that wasn't an option. Her work commitment became more cut throat as she continued to scale a steel ladder which no longer had soft cushioned rungs, but once she'd identified the difference between those two outlooks and perspectives, separated by three thousand miles of ocean, she felt more confident of succeeding.

Her day usually began in similar fashion to an Antelope awakening to the sound of gunfire. The first job of the morning was to make the bathrooms before anyone else, if only to guarantee she made it downstairs for breakfast, which was always the main meal, being as opportunity to eat food during the remainder of the day was a rarity. Sometimes she got lucky and managed to smuggle a banana or other piece of fruit into her ballet bag before disappearing to catch the subway.

Once Julie arrived at DTH it would be straight into company ballet class for approximately one and a half hours, then the dancers would break off for fifteen minutes before studying and learning the repertoire the company intended to take on their next tour, or were using for their next performance in New York. The usual yearly calendar consisted of a one week season at a local theatre and then the rest of the year free to tour the States and outside world.

The day soon came when Julie finally met Arthur Mitchell for the first time at the DTH. She was busy in the dance studio, going through a number of warming up exercises in an atmosphere which was usually sedate and calm at that time of the morning. That was until a loud, intimidating voice sounding off from somewhere below the stairs, made everyone straighten bolt upright. Then he appeared in the doorway, both eyes on fire, with a presence which totally oozed with intimidation.

Arthur Mitchell strode across the floor, as if he'd just purchased the large grand piano, used by the pianist during the ballet classes, at an overpriced sale. Then suddenly, he turned and glared across the room directly at Julie.

"Ah, the English girl has decided to join us," he mocked.

She could have answered back with the same level of sarcasm, but decided not to and just stood there, looking sheepish, not wanting to rock this particular tyrant's boat. But Mitchell didn't follow up with more verbal punching. Instead he began to teach the class, making those who he regarded as subordinates feel as though they were novices attending his class for the very first time.

Julie found her new mentor's teaching alien to all she had learned before. Throughout the lesson, Mitchell threw taunts of discomfort at his new recruit, keeping her in her place, constantly reminding her of who the master was. It appeared that in his eyes, she could not do anything right, nor would she. His infernal yelling echoed throughout the building.

"English girl, that's not right."

"English girl, what in God's name do you think you're doing?"

"English girl, have you come here to dance or to prance?"

Stuff you, Mister bloody Mitchell.

By the end of her first day with Arthur Mitchell, Julie could hardly walk, let alone do a few high kicking movements. On her way home that night, she fell to sleep as the subway train rattled and caressed her like a mother would her child in a cradle.

After dinner, she inspected her feet, as was the daily routine for a professional dancer. The blisters on her toes, which had been hardened with surgical spirits, had freshly opened and were once again, bleeding.

So, out came the spirits, accompanied by the painful grimace across her face as she poured the burning liquid over her open wounds. She felt sick and weak, her body losing more weight each day with nervous energy now her daily companion. Nancy from Poughkeepsie proved to be a close dear friend, always worrying about Julie's health and refusing to allow her to go anywhere alone, which was comforting but at times, also restrictive. It was just a bloody shame that Nancy couldn't have possessed some remarkable God given gift for healing battered toes.

Things began to turn around, as they usually did when problems were being confronted head on by a strong willed English girl from a working class background, one who had no time for the kind of American, 'we're greater than you' bullshit, which had been constantly thrown her way. She quickly restored her confidence in the American ballet style and as for that bloody repertoire, she had breathed and lived it like no other dancer in the company. In fact, she was filled to the brim with Mitchell's ideology and practical philosophy, so much so, it seeped down the sides.

She enjoyed the occasional respite, sitting alone with her thoughts in Saint Patrick's Cathedral or taking the 'every Sunday' telephone call from her mother, in a booth in the lobby of the Webster Home for Girls, with Nancy not very far off her delicate shoulder. Doreen Felix was so hell bent on putting that new telephone to good use and both mother and daughter would spend as much time as possible exchanging and sharing whatever bits of gossip came to mind. Her boyfriend Kevin, also put in his two penny worth, at least once a week and all the calls Julie received became her life line with home, with those who genuinely cared for her.

Then one July evening, after Julie and Nancy had finished dinner and returned to their rooms, after arranging to meet up later, she was seated at the small desk, continuing a love letter to Kevin, her heart filled with emotion, when suddenly all around her went black. At first she thought she'd been struck down by some wicked virus that caused blindness. She became disorientated and felt beads of sweat trickling down her forehead, sourced by raw fear. She quickly held a hand in front of her face, but it wasn't there. Then the sounds of sirens and alarms told her the problem was coming from outside her own body and mind. Something had happened, something was going down that was at the very least, extremely serious.

She heard a commotion outside in the corridor, as a number of hysterical women passed by her door, feeling their way along the walls. There were screams, howls, incoherent words being shouted in utter frenzied delirium. Those verbal exchanges she could make out weren't exactly confidence boosting.

"We're being attacked."

"The city is under siege."

"The buildings on fire." That one shook Julie to the core and she began to sniff for smoke, unsuccessfully.

"We're going to die." That last exclamation got Julie quickly to her feet.

Slowly she felt for the door and opened it, standing motionless as torches began to appear, illuminating the corridor outside. She noticed a few of the older women were dressed in combat style uniforms, in all probability armed to the teeth like a smattering of vigilantes who had been waiting in readiness for just such an occasion. To discover what planet the invaders had travelled from was obviously a first priority. Was the planet really being invaded? There was more mayhem at the top of the staircase, as the hordes of women all tried to make for the ground floor at the same time, the lifts having been taken out of action. The whole panicky situation was bloody ridiculous with no real information forthcoming. What the hell was going down here?

Now July in Manhattan wasn't exactly the coldest month of the year and the outside temperatures had recently hit the one hundred degree mark, which thankfully, was usually dealt with by the air conditioning in virtually every building in New York. Only on that particular night the air conditioners at the Webster Home for Girls had gone caput. The heat began to take over, stifling and adding to the alarm of all the residents.

Julie decided the best way forward was not to go forward, so just sat on the floor, doing her best to avoid the clambering feet that were still heading towards the stairwell.

"Hey now, ladies, just calm yourselves," the black doorman shouted out, as he appeared on the tenth floor, having had to climb his puffing and blowing way up from the ground, with a large torch in one hand, "It's okay, there's been an electrical blackout." He advised the girls to go back to their rooms and patiently wait it out.

"Hey, Mack," one of the women screamed out, Mack being the common name used to address any American male, "You've got to be kidding us."

Most of the other ladies agreed. Unless you were carrying the same torches and other implements with which the vigilante women were equipped, reluctance to return to their rooms was an understatement. At least some kind of order had been restored and the madness involved in trying to escape subsided, replaced by calmness in the knowledge the building was not on fire, neither was New York being attacked by some alien force.

"What in hell's name you doing down there, girl," one woman asked, as she looked down at Julie, a true picture of Nazi aggression, wearing her combatants with grenades attached to each of her fully blown up boobs.

"It's cooler on the floor," Julie answered back, knowing it wasn't really.

A multitude of questions were thrown at the poor doorman who was trying his best to quell the concerns, but without much success.

Julie managed to shuffle along the semi lit corridor and reach the stairs. At first she intended to descend down the ten floors to the ground, where she could get out of the building and hopefully find cooler air, but following a few of the more mature and clearer thinking women, she finally reached the roof.

Unfortunately, the air outside was as close as that inside, so with the others, she just sat for a spell, listening to the street noises down below and hoping the situation would soon be resolved. At least she thought she'd made the right decision by making the roof. It sounded like bedlam down on the street with widespread looting, windows being smashed, guns going off and even cars crashing into God knows what. It later transpired that traffic lights had gone down and people were just abandoning their cars and hightailing it for home or any other place which offered them safety. It was all so terrifying and she pictured in her mind, a scene from some domestic uprising in the middle of a civil war. Then, covering her ears with her hands, she was just about to scream out when two arms suddenly grabbed her from behind and to her relief and ecstasy, she'd found Nancy.

The 1977 New York electricity black out lasted for two days, 13th and 14th July, during which time the city was subjected to widespread looting, arson and other pockets of disorder. Records show that in total, 1,616 stores were victims of looting and rioting, over a thousand fires were responded to by the emergency services and the largest number of arrests made in New York's history, exceeded three and a half thousand. Some people blamed the lunacy on the prolonged rising temperatures, others on wanton violence and crime, including the city's mayor at that time, Abe Beame who said,

'We've seen our citizens subjected to violence, vandalism, theft and discomfort. The Blackout has threatened our safety and has seriously impacted our economy. We've been needlessly subjected to a night of terror in many communities that have been wantonly looted and burned. The costs when finally tallied will be enormous.'

In fact, a congressional study later estimated the cost of damages amounted to more than $300 million.

Julie in Mother Goose   Julie's Grandfather (on left) the Royal Guard

Patrick and Doreen Felix

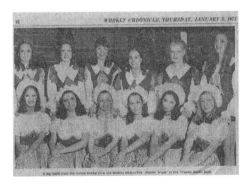

The cast of Mother Goose – Julie on front left

Mother and Daughter

Lucia and Julie (on right)

Classes and Rehearsing

Dance Theatre Harlem   Arthur Mitchell

DTH outside the Royal Opera House Covent Garden

Julie's Billboard Poster

Patrick in later life

Lucia

HAPPY: Julie Felix and Joseph Cipolla

Lifetime duet for dancers Julie and Joe

DANCER Julie Felix tomorrow performs the duet of a lifetime with her American boyfriend Joseph Cipolla.

Julie has come home to West Ealing from New York with Joe to get married.

The happy couple, both stars with the world-famous Dance Theatre of Harlem, will be exchanging vows at St Aidan's United Reformed Church in Northfield Avenue.

Julie, who is staying with Joe at her parents' home in Cranmer Avenue, said: "We are so happy. It's wonderful to be able to come home to get married."

The couple met when Joe, 23, joined the theatre almost five years ago.

Julie, 27, who started dancing with the Joyce Butler School in Ealing, had already been with the company a year.

The theatre has a heavy schedule which means Joe, Julie and their fellow dancers are often away touring. They have just returned from a tour of Japan.

She has been so busy this is the first time her mum Doreen, 61, and Dad Patrick, 65, a retired Hoover worker, have seen her for two years.

After a honeymoon in Devon Julie and Joe fly back to America to spend a week with his parents, who live in New York state.

Julie's Joe

162

Chapter Eighteen

First Performance

Following that historical and traumatic series of events, Julie's mother was forever on the phone, understandably worried for her daughter's safety, but Doreen Felix's concerns were unfounded as the young black ballet dancer took everything in her stride. After all, Julie was there to learn and progress, but one particular change in her way of thinking was slowly evolving. As she was becoming more accustomed to the American way of life, she was also distancing herself from her English boyfriend, Kevin.

She knew that the good looking shark fisherman from Cornwall, was still plodding along without any kind of direction in his life and sadly it appeared to Julie that he never would have. Good old Kevin hadn't bothered to save up any money to visit his girlfriend in New York, as he had solemnly promised, therefore in this case, absence didn't make the heart grow fonder and his presence in his girlfriend's mind was beginning to fade. His main competitor, Julie's love for the Ballet, was winning hands down.

The Dance Theatre Harlem, like most ballet companies, had their own residential theatre at which they would perform when not on tour. For at least a one week season each year, the company would dance at the City Centre Theatre in Manhattan and that year's booking was the first opportunity for Julie to perform as a true professional. It would be the first time she danced in front of a live audience since Nureyev's Sleeping Beauty and she longed for the day when it would happen.

She became more apprehensive as the venue drew nearer; taking some encouragement from the rest of the company's confident, if not laid back attitudes. Obviously they had all been there before, had all driven around the block many times and to them, training and rehearsing were far more difficult than actually performing live.

The theatre was situated on West 55th Street, not far from the famous Carnegie Hall and Julie, who was brimming over with enthusiasm, made the usual subway ride, carrying a new, much larger ballet bag filled with her practice clothing, ballet shoes and a whole heap of new stage make-up, which she had been advised to purchase. It was the odour from those oily substances in that thickly painted make-up, that brought back fond memories of watching her mother prepare for her operatic singing recitals, Doreen Felix's little girl's face forever displaying the fantasy and magical wonderment of the theatre.

When on stage, the performer always had to accentuate real life appearances, the eyes being given stronger eye liner, eye shadow, false eye lashes and deep red lipstick. Julie's hair would always be literally scraped back into a high bun on the crown of her head and sealed into place with hairspray, pins, clips and hair net. There was no doubt, that new ballet bag, bulging to its limit, had become a necessity.

In addition to each dancer's personal equipment, they were all provided with what was referred to as a black box, in which several additional ballet shoes would be stored away, including performance tights and other items usually too heavy to carry. The company would be responsible for transporting the black boxes, but on that first occasion at the City Centre Theatre, Julie hadn't yet been allocated a black box, so everything she owned had to find room inside that oversized dance bag, which seemed to dwarf its owner. By the time she would reach the theatre there should be an empty black box waiting for her in which she could unload.

The City Centre Theatre was unusual in appearance with its flat front and green domed roof, having been first built in 1923 as a Mecca Temple for the Ancient Arabic Order of the Nobles of the Mystic Shrine. Some title for a private club whose members, known as the Shriners, had been thrown out of their previous meeting place as a result of all the cigar smoke they used to leave behind them.

After arriving at the theatre, Julie entered through the stage door and signed in, noticing there was a distinct lack of cigar smoke around the place. There was a board prominently displayed though, containing a list of all the dancers and the dressing room numbers assigned to each one. The corps de ballet, in which Julie was a member, always shared dressing rooms in groups of six and as her heartbeat began to test her ribcage, she quickly found her name. So, it wasn't up there in lights, but by God, it looked really good and from now on, she would be justified in telling any person enquiring as to the nature of her employment, she was a professional, experienced ballet dancer. Just wait until she was endowed with the true label of Ballerina.

Reality soon came back to her when another girl from the company touched her shoulder and spoke softly, "Hi Julie, ready for the performance of your life? You're in the same dressing room as me, so come on, let's go and find your black box."

It didn't take long to come across forty odd black boxes all lined up against a wall, each with a name boldly printed thereon, except one, which was obviously Julie's and was found to be empty. Far from being disappointed, she knew that situation would soon be resolved, so with ballet bag in one hand and the empty black box in the other, she made her way to the appropriate dressing room.

She found the door open and was warmly greeted by three other female members of the company. Mind you, it was a case of every girl for herself when it came to choosing a spot to park up. Julie then sat and watched like an inquisitive child seeing something for the first time, as the others began to unpack. Each girl had about five pairs of ballet tights, three or four leotards, leg warmers, sweat shirts, five or six pairs of pointe shoes and several pairs of flats, ballet shoes without the pointes. It was like attending a church jumble sale and after everything had been spread out, there wasn't much room left for the humans to move about in.

The girls' make up bags were the biggest Julie had ever cast her eyes on, containing face cleanser, shower gel, creams and just about everything else except the kitchen sink. In fact, one of the girls used to carry a small kettle for emergencies. It wouldn't be long when Julie's black box would be filled with the same paraphernalia, of that she had no doubt.

They all congregated on the stage for that opening day's first rehearsal and company class and Julie watched and mimicked everything the other dancers did, muddling her way through the various exercises. It felt strange, finally performing on a real life stage and although she felt like a fish out of water, the experience was exhilarating. Portable ballet barres had been set up and the fire curtain had been raised to show off the three thousand empty seats in the auditorium, which they all learned later had been sold out for the forthcoming season of performances, their performances. In fact, most of DTHs performances were to sell out audiences.

Later in her career, Julie would discover that every theatre is different in some respects, but also special in others. For instance, when there was no audience, a coldness seemed to descend on the auditorium, an eerie kind of atmosphere that couldn't be easily explained. That didn't bother the girl from Ealing much and it was something she got used to, aware that such an experience made the live audience performances even more exciting and spectacular.

As she did her warming up exercises she took time to look out at the emptiness of a theatre that was full of beauty and elegance, trying hard to guess at what the atmosphere would be like on opening night, with virtually three thousand paying people staring back at her from the darkness. She quickly returned to earth when three ladies began hoovering the floors.

Although Julie felt calm during those initial exercises and rehearsals, she also knew that wouldn't be the case once the show opened.

"Okay, people, let's begin," shouted her boss, indicating Mister Mitchell was ready to begin teaching the class.

It was all so new, all so thrilling, all so adventurous and exciting. The stage rehearsal the following day would include the dress rehearsal and every single dancer was looking forward to that one, including Julie.

She had already met the head of wardrobe, Miss Wynn, when having her costume fittings, a small black lady with heavy spectacles who used to wear a wig and appeared to be around eighty years of age, although people told Julie that Miss Wynn had been around eighty ever since the company first started rolling. Some of the others warned the youngest member of the company to ensure she hung up her costume correctly at the end of each performance, otherwise she would feel the little old lady's wrath. They were spot on; after each performance, the piercing eyes of Miss Wynn would scan every costume, in similar fashion to a drill sergeant inspecting the troops and if she found anything not to her liking, then the recipient of a tidal wave of verbal abuse would wish they'd joined the army instead.

Chapter Nineteen

Fire on 34th Street

This was to be a very special day, the one she had dreamed of throughout her childhood, during the three years at Rambert and ever since arriving in New York; the day she would be highlighting in her diary, recording implicit details of her first live performance. At five o'clock that same morning however, the dream was almost completely wrecked.

Julie awoke with a start and the smell of smoke was strong. She leapt from her bed and switched the light on, but there was no sign, just that acrid smell. The building was on fire, she had no doubt, but where? She opened the door of her room, half expecting to be greeted by flames leaping towards her, but there was nothing except darkness and silence. She turned and stepped across to the window and there saw the source of her anxiety, just across the way, in the apartment block opposite.

A young man, as naked as a Jay bird was hanging from the sill of an open window, grasping the ledge desperately as flames and smoke seemed to be searching for him, just above where his head was moving up and down, spinning around in frenzied defiance.

She could hear the trapped man's terrifying screams and calls for help, his struggling body seemingly covered in black soot, as he just hung there, unable to make the fire escape which was being closely guarded by the licking flames. Clouds of black smoke enveloped his body, making him barely visible and slowly filling his lungs with all kinds of chemical nasties. It would only be a matter of seconds before the poor man would become asphyxiated or decided he'd had enough, either way the result would be the same and he would fall to his inevitable death.

Julie's first thought was to dial 911 but by the time she made the phone booth on the ground floor, it would be too late. Then in the far distance she heard the sound of wailing sirens and jerked her window open as the emergency services drew nearer. All she could do now was yell at the trapped nudist, giving him what she thought would be welcome news, that the fire fighters were on their way. Being all of ten storeys up from the ground, she guessed the man would be hoping they'd bring a bloody long ladder with them, plus a few gallons of water.

As with most emergencies, when those willing to give a hand to someone else subjected to a life threatening crisis, time always seemed to slow down, everything being counted in seconds. In the same way as when you're driving in one hell of a hurry to get somewhere and find yourself sitting behind a farm tractor doing no more than ten miles an hour, unable to be passed. But Julie still shouted out, doing her best to offer words of encouragement, trying hard not to say anything that might make the poor man decide to jump, rather than rely on the city's brigade,

"Don't worry, in a few minutes, you will be toast and the problem would have been sorted."

No, nothing like that, more like, "Just hang on, feller, not long now, they'll soon have you down," which would have been a lot more reassuring if it wasn't for those scorching flames leaping around his head. Whether her words reached him was anyone's guess, but after what seemed like hours, but were probably a few minutes of life threatening tension, the boys with the yellow helmets arrived and were soon chasing up a ladder, the property of the New York Fire Department. And, just like in the conclusion of a great action movie, after wrapping the frightened young man in the usual foil blanket, supposedly invented by NASA, an angry back draft decided to take out the window frame completely by exploding and leaping skywards, over the very spot where the victim had been dangling from just a few seconds before. Two more of New York's finest came up the ladder, each armed with hoses and began to extinguish the flames. No one could have wished for a more dramatic ending, but of course, this wasn't the end bit of a movie, this was real and the whole business left Julie feeling totally shot through and completely bowled over.

She stood for a moment or two, staring across at that black hole, which had once been an apartment window, her body trembling, having just seen a young innocent man shake hands with death, missing out on being one more of the city's fatalities by just a few seconds. That was most certainly very scary and for once she had seen someone else take on some of those heavy knockout punches life had a habit of throwing at the human race. What more could this city of cities offer her in the form of fear and traumatic reality?

It wasn't supposed to have happened this way on the very day she would be preparing for her first night in front of a live audience. She was supposed to have breakfasted nice and early, taken her time making the theatre and going through the day's dress rehearsal, calmly and at ease with the world. Now, thanks to the man in the charcoal suit, she had missed her breakfast and the clock was telling her it was time to shift her rear end more quickly than she had ever done before. Everything required was dumped into her bag and the race began in earnest.

The journey was blessed by Guardian Angels, as the train came in just as Julie was flying down the platform.

"Hey, sister, where you going?" had been completely ignored and once she had arrived at the other end, she took off again, moving faster than even Sebastian Coe, before finally making her destination, gasping for breath with both arms feeling like lead weights, which was no way to feel before starting on the most important itinerary in her life thus far. But she was young, strong and able, or so she kept telling herself as she threw everything down, got changed quicker than Superman in a telephone box and spun down the corridor, joining the rest of the company on stage.

There was an unwritten ruling that applied to every member of the company, a sort of invisible charter that declared no one was allowed to arrive after Arthur Mitchell had entered to take his class. Julie made it by a hair's breadth and was standing at the barre when everyone called out,

"Good morning, Mister Mitchell."

"Right, people, let's begin."

There are those who believe if the rehearsals go well, then the actual performances will suffer, but Julie didn't necessarily feel that way. The dress rehearsal did go well, with Arthur Mitchell sitting in the auditorium, with the house lights down, so none of the dancers could actually see him, his vocal instructions bellowing out over a microphone he used to nurse on his lap. The Dance Theatre Harlem had a staff of sixty five people, forty of them dancers, the rest being lighting technicians, wardrobe people and so on. All of these non-dancing members took advantage of the dress rehearsal by adjusting lights, costumes and whatever else was required.

Much to Julie's disappointment, Arthur Mitchell dropped the habit of calling her, 'English girl,' and became more impersonal by addressing his youngest member by her surname.

"Felix, get into line."

"Felix, what the hell do you think you're doing," and so on.

After rehearsals on that final day, the company were allowed to take a one hour break, between 5.30 p.m. and 6.30 p.m. being required to return to the theatre one hour before curtain for make-up and one last half hour ballet class. At 7.0 p.m. the final call would be made, 'half an hour before curtain'.

Whether or not the company felt confident, which was usually the case, each dancer had their own small idiosyncrasies, which included placing ballet shoes in a certain way while dressing; some would cross themselves before each performance, others organised their costumes in a special way. It was all intended to calm the nerves and add a big dose of psychological support. During that final half hour, what had been checked already would be checked again. Final adjustments to the angle of lighting in the wings and those inside the auditorium would be made. Costumes tweaked to perfection, make-up scrutinised and final warm up exercises completed.

At 7.15 p.m. a quarter of an hour to curtain, the stage manager would bawl out, "Places please." That was it, no more tweaking or leg movements. The first ballet was about to begin and the next stage in the proceedings would be the striking up of the orchestra, just before the curtain lifted and the performance began.

For the whole of that particular one week season, the company was to perform a triple bill, beginning with the *Holberg Suite* by Grieg, which would last approximately forty minutes, followed by 'Forces of Rhythm' and finally, 'Dougla'.

So, the dancers waited anxiously, nerve ends tingling, beads of sweat already beginning to make their way down so many flexible spines, everyone feeling the edge. Then the orchestra began to play and slowly the curtain raised, revealing a blanket of darkness from which there came applause. Julie took a short involuntary gasp of air as the heat of the lighting began to pour down on the cast. But she was ready, so was everyone else, thank God.

The odd few coughs from the darkness of the auditorium was the only indication to the dancers that there was a sell out crowd watching their performance. Otherwise, the only sound in the building came from the well-tuned orchestra.

Julie played her role well, flying through the air with ease, style and grace, like an imp chasing her shadow. She danced her heart out, completely focused on giving the demonstration of her life. She felt she wanted to dance larger than life itself and thought of her mother's wonderful singing voice, wishing she could have borrowed it, if only for that night. Her out of body experience took her floating away from all of life's tribulations, strangely watching herself excel with natural ability and artistic acumen, all coming together as she played out her role.

At the conclusion of the first ballet, the audience applauded madly, six thousand hands all clapping at once, with shouts of 'bravo' echoing around the building. But there was no time to dwell on the plaudits and the dancers quickly disappeared back to the dressing rooms, with just fifteen minutes to change costumes, even their hairstyles, before the next performance was due to start.

The second ballet, 'Forces of Rhythm', was as exciting, graceful and artistic as the first and pride began to flow through the dancers, knowing their performances were special, a little bit more than anticipated. Mr. Mitchell would be pleased with this night's performance and his youngest girl was full of enthusiasm, delight and anticipation that she would receive some of the accolades for what she considered an outstanding interpretation. Applause followed the end of the second ballet in similar fashion to the first.

The third ballet, 'Dougla' again excelled in all of its movements, the dancers continuing with their magnificent and enthralling rendition. Although the heat from the lights was immense and energy sapping,

Julie felt as if she could have continued dancing throughout the night. All the girl's most inner distressing concerns about the colour of her skin and being away from home in a strange country had left her, only the thrill of the moment mattered. Time itself had stopped and all was forgotten during that magnetic experience. At the end of that final dance, where others felt exhausted, Julie's energy levels were still going through the roof and she didn't want to stop.

The orchestra was silent and there was an eerie pause, without any kind of sound, just an awesome stillness in the auditorium. Then, like a sudden clap of thunder, the building shook as the audience gave a standing ovation, stamping their feet in appreciation and continuing to shout their encouragement with, "bravo, bravo."

Julie felt her whole body quiver with excitement, charges of electricity running from head to toe, knowing she was one of those who had earned such a response of sheer pleasure and gratitude. The night had been a success, but to Julie Felix it had also been mesmerising, magical, the height of her short professional career with add-ons. She skipped and sang her way back to the dressing room, more than happy to acknowledge a few pats on the back from the other dancers. Julie Felix from Ealing, London had finally arrived and she wondered how long it would be before she became a principle dancer, given the freedom of the stage to perform her amazing artistic talents and forgetting this was only her first performance.

Chapter Twenty

The San Gennaro Festival

It was Arthur Mitchell's usual practice to discuss the night's performances at rehearsals the following day, but on this night he chose to visit the dressing rooms. Staring directly across at Julie, the master pronounced his personal verdict of her performance.

"What the hell was that, Julie? You were never in line. You are supposed to be in the corps de ballet, which means you do not dance on your own, you must stay in line like the rest." It was all that was needed to extinguish her lights, bring her back down to earth with a bump, a short rebuke that dug into her very soul, a steaming lava flow that basically floored her.

She had danced with abandonment and enjoyment, but now felt as if her whole world had suddenly exploded and been engulfed by burning flames, the same as what she'd seen earlier that morning when that young man had just barely cheated death. From the overjoyed woman with eyes sparkling with success, she was now a deflated has been, feeling like a balloon full of hydrogen which had just been burst by a pin.

She left the theatre, not wanting to go with the others to a nearby bar to celebrate, with her head hung low and tears in her eyes. Now, her body ached; now her energy levels had suddenly become exhausted; now she felt as if all she wanted was to catch a bus to the moon and possibly beyond.

After the crestfallen female idol had experienced a sleepless night, tormenting herself with what kind of hostility she could throw back at Arthur Mitchell, following his onslaught of abuse about her first live performance, logic and common sense returned, just as the greyness of the morning sky began to filter through into her room. Should she just give it all in and return home to her mom? That would be easy, but it would also mean the end of everything she had dreamed of since she was a child. Above all, she knew deep down, that wasn't what Arthur Mitchell wanted.

Mitchell had been given an opportunity to become the first black ballet dancer in the United States by the talented George Balanchine and had formed the Dance Theatre Harlem to give other black dancers that same opportunity. Yes, he was a hard task master, probably the hardest in the business, but Julie realised his dressing down after last night's performance was for her own good. There was no doubting his true intention now in the cold light of day it was to make her the best black ballet dancer she could possibly become. So, now armed with that belief, her decision was simple; she would continue listening and taking notice of his barks and grumbles and advice, none of which she knew held any personal malice. After all, he was the master; she was still a novice trying to learn all she could. Grow up, girl; there could not be any better teacher in the world as far as she was concerned. So, Arthur Mitchell, once again became, Mr. Mitchell.

As she sat on the edge of her bed, watching the early morning sunrise, it was all so simple, she had to strip her mind of all the negatives and replace them with positive thoughts that were all logical and supported by reality. It was no longer all about Julie's dream, but the dreams of everyone else at DTH, a fact she must never again forget. And that was what Mitchell was all about.

Mind you, the criticisms didn't end on that first night. Every performance she gave throughout the remainder of that week at the City Centre Theatre, were an improvement on the last and Mr. Mitchell was always ready to hand down snipes and brick bats after each performance or at rehearsal the following day. Forget the roar of applause the company received after every triple bill, the grueling schedule continued with a ballet class for at least an hour and half each day, rehearsals until 5.30 p.m. followed by a short break, then another half hour class until the 7.0 p.m. half hour to curtain call. Every Saturday and Sunday there would be two performances a day, which meant participating in one class followed by a live performance at 2.30 p.m. and a repeat of the same in readiness for the 7.30 p.m. on stage production.

There exists an unseen, unknown force that drives artists who possess the deepest passion for what they love and they have to tap into that inner strength, courage and determination to continue, ensuring all three elements never leave them and remain their closest friends. Julie had developed those personal assets, her character was strong enough to endure the most difficult of tasks and she did continue, like a steam locomotive running full belt without taking on water. Failure was never an option, a belief she'd caught off her infectious American colleagues.

Following the engagements at the City Centre Theatre, her working life began to return to some kind of normality. In September of every year the Little Italy district in down town Manhattan, always put on a popular Italian Food Festival known as the San Gennaro Festival. The annual event is a celebration of the Patron Saint of Naples and was first held in New York in 1926. Italian immigrants focus their celebrations on Mulberry Street, inside the Italian quarter. People from all over the States attend to join in the festivities beneath hordes of Italian flags and bunting and 1977 was the year in which Julie found herself amongst the thousands of people celebrating, together with her friend, Nancy.

Although the festival was a religious one, romance was always present in the air, with young male eyes adoring female faces and figures. Everyone there under the age of eighty, felt it. It was a culmination of fantasy and dreams, love and excitement, the time for the boys to hold their shoulders back, tuck in their stomachs and arch their eyebrows and for the girls to hold their chins up high and walk in a way their mothers would have condemned.

So be it, as the two girls slowly maneuvered their way through the crowds they felt the kind of excitement and chivalry that made them giggle and laugh out loud. It wasn't very long before the inevitable happened and Julie was approached by a young, handsome Italian boy, whose interest in her was immediate and unrelenting. Oh yes, he had his shoulders back and eyebrows arched, displaying his plumage like a New Guinea Bird of Paradise.

Following a short period of verbal rapport, small snippets of conversation was exchanged between them, Julie told the Romeo with the blue eyes where she lived, not believing that she would be at risk inside the Webster House for Girls with that huge black doorman and those highly trained commando women with the overgrown boobs and always ready for war to break out. Who the hell would be capable of getting past that lot?

Her friend blew a fuse, telling Julie she was never to talk to strange men in New York, but she remained unmoved and the day passed by without any unwelcome incident. During the following day, when everyone was seated for dinner at the Webster House, the communications system announced there was a telephone call for room 1006. She knew it couldn't be a call from England because it was a weekday and the only person who made a call on any day except the weekend was Kevin from Truro, and he'd been long dispatched. The rest of the girls were also aware of that and as Julie approached the handset on the wall, she felt the heavy breathing of fifty of the other women, who had followed her out of the dining room.

A cheer went up after the telephone call had ended and Julie announced to the gathering that she had been invited out on Saturday by Joe, the Italian Stallion. Good for you, Julie.

Chapter Twenty-One

Winter

Joe, the Italian hunk, had the same mind set as Julie's previous boyfriends. It seemed that as soon as a member of the male species found out the girl who had taken their fancy was in fact a professional ballerina, they became intoxicated with the idea that their date glided across the boards, entertaining the aristocracy, which of course wasn't the case, but that was the image Classical Ballet gave to the uninitiated. So, Julie and Joe became a pair of misfits, although happy with each other's company. She was from Ealing, London and possessed a vast amount of artistic talent, he from Brooklyn, New York, without a spec of artistic interest in his brain. And the huge Atlantic Ocean that separated their places of birth, didn't matter a hoot. He was just as proud of his heritage and country as Julie and intended to demonstrate such loyalty to both the Stars and Stripes and Red, Green and White Italian standard.

Neither was Joe the kind of bloke who was slow to get his feet under the table, quickly acting as the perfect escort when he whizzed his new found romance around his city, with one objective in mind, for her to see how real New Yorkers lived. He had two itineraries, a list of places where tourists and visitors didn't frequent, and some of the more well-known locations graced by legal aliens and just about everybody else. Whenever an opportunity prevailed, they travelled at such breakneck speed, Julie's delicate toes didn't touch the ground, stopping at just about every back street and unfamiliar restaurant or store known to mankind, where at least prices of items remained stable and you didn't have to pay for the guy with the violin serenading you as you ate your Spaghetti Bolognaise.

She quickly learned that New Yorkers worked hard and played hard in the Big Apple, experiencing all aspects of life in the city and to the naïve black girl from England, what a way of life that was. She was finally beginning to understand why fate had brought her to this Land of the Free, America, a continent that had opened its arms to embrace her natural talents, no matter what the colour of her skin happened to be. Her love affair with the country itself began in earnest, but she still felt like a schizophrenic, unable to drop the burning torch she held for her home back in Ealing.

The real surprise package came when Joe took the girl for dinner at a restaurant situated a hundred floors up in one of the World Trade Centres, sparking an experience that would remain in her memory for the rest of her life. After making the one hundredth floor they were met with a severe electrical storm with the night sky filled with bolts and streaks of lightning, dramatically flashing across a black background, in similar fashion to a fireworks display at the closing ceremony of an Olympic Games. Claps of thunder could be heard outside, giving the impression that God himself was applauding the young couple for having made it up the elevator. Thus, the romance of that evening was enhanced further and their relationship strengthened by nature itself. More importantly, following that particular excursion, Joe became amazingly relaxed and agreeable with Julie's constant need to dance, eat and sleep.

The ballerina's first Christmas away from home was full of joy and sadness as the impulsive yearnings which kept drawing her thoughts back to home refused to subside, leaving her on occasions, utterly devastated. The communications system boomed once more at Webster House, informing everyone that there was a large parcel for 1006 and Julie hurried down the ten floors, knowing her Christmas box from home had arrived.

After carrying the package back up to her room she opened it with tears already welling up her eyes. Inside, she found a variety of her favourite English treats, Chocolate Digestives, Earl Grey tea and various selections of Cadbury chocolates. It was strange how such delicacies created so much anger and frustration, having to be so far away from home at that one time in the year when families met and celebrated together, only because of her love for ballet.

Julie strongly felt she'd been the victim of bullying, cast aside by her own country for one reason only, not that she wasn't good enough or didn't have sufficient talent to turn professional, but only because she was black, because segregation had seemed to be the order of the day, fashionable in that time, people rejecting other human beings, not because they didn't like them, but more like sheep feeling the need to follow their fellow man. Julie was convinced that racism in her own country came more from habit and being part of the status quo than any personal malice. Nobody wanted a black swan in a white swan line and those bloody hypocrites would never have given her a second thought. At least the New York weather was about to add some cheer to her depression.

The winter of that year was one of the worst the city had experienced, with heavy snow bringing Manhattan to a total shut down. In similar fashion to a city dweller suddenly awakening in the countryside only to find the silence deafening, Julie rejoined the living one early morning and immediately missed the usual sounds of wailing sirens and honking horns down in the street. All was silent, peaceful, and tranquil. She rushed to the window and gazed out at an oasis of white blankets covering as far as the eye could see. Almost twenty foot of snow had fallen while the city had slept.

Wall Street, the subway, the emergency services had all taken refuge and was at a standstill. Unlike the blackout, there was no looting or disorder, no criminal rampaging, after all, how would any light fingered New Yorker escape with every vehicle incapable of movement and where would they go with their stolen bounty?

It was inevitable that the vigilante women would don on their garbs, kitting themselves out with commando style clothing, boots and utility belts, just in case an alien attacking force had been responsible for the freak weather. Even Nancy, who had been used to snow in Poughkeepsie announced with sincerity, she had never seen the likes of this before. That only encouraged the vigilantes to march up and down the corridors with eyes scanning for every insect and spider's movement.

When Julie finally ventured outside into the frosty air, she could see that lamp posts and traffic signals had disappeared under the 'white out,' people were actually skiing up Fifth Avenue, all newcomers to the streets greeting each other with joy, love and equality, as if the President had declared a national holiday. Mind you, that might have been the case, as no one was going to work that day and all were in the same boat, rowing in the same direction, no work but plenty of play for the minions. It reminded her of a scene from Dicken's Christmas Carol, except there was no Scrooge anywhere in sight.

As the days flew past, leaving abandoned heaps of snow on just about every street corner, the city began to mobilise again, normality beginning to creep in like an invading army. At the Dance Theatre Harlem things were definitely getting back to normality, as one season ends another rehearsal period begins. The dancers way of life there, always reminded Julie of a conveyor belt that must continue running in order for the produce to drop into the basket at the other end.

Every morning Julie was the first in the studio, completing her warm up exercises before the first class began. On one particular morning, Arthur Mitchell walked in and told Julie he needed to speak with her after class, which had an immediate nauseating affect on his youngest dancer. Was he going to send her home? Had she not reached his required standard? Had she let herself and England down and was now about to see her dreams vanquished, having to land at Heathrow with her head bowed in shame and a vale of sadness and depression hanging over her? Most of all, had she let her parents down after spending all that money to help carve a pathway of success for their daughter? Once again, her dishevelled mind began to spin in different directions.

The co-director, Karl Shook, took the company class that morning, but Julie was so pre-occupied with dreading what lay in store for her, that she faltered for the first time, more than once.

"Julie, concentrate, what the hell are you doing," Karl Shook shouted across the studio floor. She tried harder, but couldn't stop thinking bad thoughts, like a person awaiting sentence to be passed, a death sentence, 'And you will be taken from here to a place of execution where you will be hanged by your neck until you are dead, and may the Lord have mercy on your soul, woman.'

The end of the lesson came quickly enough and she left her towel and pointe shoes in the studio, an absence of mind that was certainly uncommon. She stood for a moment before the main man's door, hesitant and fearing what was to happen on the other side. She knocked and a voice told her to enter, which she did. At the far end of the room, Arthur Mitchell sat behind a large, heavily built solid oak desk and watched as Julie slowly walked towards him before standing there like a three year old about to be scorned.

"Right now, Julie," he actually called her for the very first time by her Christian name, which was ominous in itself, "Mister Shook and I have given this a lot of thought..."

What time was the flight back to London, she thought, her lower lip beginning to quiver.

"And we have decided to begin the process of getting you a Green Card."

She had no idea what a Green Card was and wondered whether it was some sort of final warning for her to pull her socks up. At least she would still have a job with the company.

"We have had to put an advertisement in the New York Times stating that we are looking to employ a female dancer for a full contract with DTH," he continued, "But, obviously we would not be looking for a female dancer really, because we have you and both of us have agreed we want you to have the job, but legally we have to go through the process of advertising."

She was well aware that it would cost the company several thousand dollars to legally get a full time contract for anyone and what Mitchell was telling her, was that they wanted to spend that money on Julie Felix. "So, I need to know if you want the job?"

Well, at first she was speechless, a million thoughts raced through her mind. It meant her plans to return to England during the forthcoming summer and apply for an English company would be dashed. Her greatest dilemma, though, was thinking that she had been asked to marry someone she didn't love. The signs were there for the marriage to be successful, but something was missing and the thought of being exiled dug deeply. Then Angela Ellis's advice came to mind, "Never turn down a job, darling."

"Well?" he asked.

"Thank you, Mr. Mitchell, yes I really want to join your company."

"Good," he said, before turning back to the paperwork on his desk, which was his way of saying, 'Now, go away, girl.'

PART FOUR

On Tour

Chapter Twenty-Two

Arthur Mitchell

Following her lucrative meeting with Arthur Mitchell, Julie soon found herself sitting alone in St Patrick's Cathedral, allowing her thoughts to pick up on her latest exhilarating news, her mind searching the depths like a radar scanner. She'd travelled thousands of miles and worked bloody hard to land that contract, of that there was no doubt. She felt worthy of such an accolade and nobody could take that away from her now. Did it really matter that this had happened in America? No, not really she told herself, so why hold on so tightly to all those memories of home and a constant burning desire to return as soon as possible. Above all, it had taken a man who had also been persecuted because of his colour, to give her this wonderful opportunity.

Arthur Mitchell knew all about poverty and fighting for survival, which was probably the reason he was such a dedicated, hard task manager of those he employed. He had been born and raised on the streets of Harlem and his family's circumstances meant the young Arthur had to grow up fast. He worked from an early age to help his family make ends meet, shining shoes, mopping floors, working in a meat shop and delivering newspapers. No matter how low or poorly paid the offer was, he always took the job.

When just a young teenager, Mitchell was encouraged to apply successfully to the High School of Performing Arts where he excelled in Classical Ballet, before winning a scholarship to the School of American Ballet. Encouraged and supported by the Russian Choreographer, George Balanchine, Mitchell made his debut in 1955 as the first black American ballet dancer with the New York City Ballet and from that time, the lad from Harlem never looked back.

He remained as the only black dancer with that company for many years, and one highlight of his career was performing the pas de deux in Agon, created especially for Mitchell and the white ballerina, Diana Adams, by Balanchine. Although he danced the role with a number of white partners throughout the world, ironically the American television networks refused to cover the performance before 1965, only because the Southern States, including Mississippi, refused to carry it.

Eventually, he left the New York City Ballet in 1966 to appear in several shows on Broadway before returning to Harlem with an overwhelming desire to create similar opportunities he'd been blessed with, to other talented kids struggling on the streets of the black communities. Hence he created the Dance Theatre Harlem, together with his old teacher, Karl Shook. Mitchell put in $25,000 of his own money to start the company and within a year had secured £315,000 from the Ford Foundation.

DTH began its life in a church basement with 30 youngsters participating, which quickly increased to over 400 attending classes. By 1971 the company was ready to present their first production as a professional company, which was successful and launched an ever increasing popularity with the public.

It was ironic that after leaving the cathedral, Julie walked along Fifth Avenue until she came to an elegant looking antique shop, where she suddenly stopped and gazed at an item on display in the window. It was an old green couch, a replica of the one located in the basement at Rambert. Surely, this couldn't be the same green couch she and Mary had spent so much time with, subjecting themselves to all that tortuous training, could it? The shop was closed so she couldn't find out where the green couch had come from, but then suddenly realised, with a heavy heart, that she'd actually forgotten the smaller details of the Rambert couch and that dreams and wishful thinking were now becoming more prominent than reality.

She had grown up since those days and was now a mature, adult ballerina; a swan that had evolved from the cygnet whose body had been developed and trained in readiness for what she was about to embark on. She also knew that she had to finally let go of the sadness of having not danced professionally in her own country and concentrate more on becoming the best English black ballerina in America. She truly had to count her blessings.

As soon as she got back to Webster House she telephoned her mother, telling her of the events that had taken place during that day. At first there was a lengthy pause, her mother obviously coming to terms with the fact that her daughter would not be coming home that summer, but then happiness and congratulations which made Julie feel like a million dollars.

Soon afterwards, in the Spring of 1978, the Dance Theatre Harlem went on tour. It was Julie's first trip out of New York after being told to pack a suitcase because she would be on the road for about three weeks. Sometimes the company would travel by bus, on other occasions, they flew to their destinations and some of the locations visited included, St Louis, Idaho, Mississippi, Iowa, Ohio, Missouri, Alabama and New Orleans. It was all adventurous for the young English girl and exciting as the company always performed to packed audiences in some of the grandest theatres in the States.

The company's first engagement was in St Louis but they were greeted by one of the heaviest rainfalls the city had known. Streets became flooded and Julie watched as abandoned cars floated around like lost sheep looking for shelter from the tremendous downpours, wondering whether all of these freak record breaking weather conditions had followed her across the Atlantic. Of course, the inevitable happened and the performance in St Louis was quickly cancelled, leaving the company stranded in their hotel, but the dancers took everything in their stride and enjoyed the break from training and rehearsals.

The Domino Pizza Company had delivery facilities all over the States and as a group, the stranded dancers decided to test the Domino promise not to charge for any pizza ordered and not delivered piping hot within one hour. They all placed bets on various times in which their order would be delivered, if delivered at all and agreeing the winner would get theirs free of charge. So the order was placed and the clock began ticking.

"I'm surprised they even took the order in this weather," said one of the males.

"How the hell are they going to get to us through these floods," said another.

All eyes were fixed on the debris that was floating past the front of the hotel when suddenly one of the girls called out, "My God, there he is, he's coming."

It was an amazing sight to see a boy coming up the street, through two feet of running water, wearing waders and a load of hot piping pizzas held high above his head. The bet was well won and each member of the company laughed their socks off.

"This beats rehearsals," said one.

"I'm not so sure about that," said another, "Just don't let Mr. Mitchell hear you."

During Julie's first year at DTH, there weren't any union ties, although some of the bigger ballet companies worked with the AGMA union which was similar to Equity, the union for actors and artists in Great Britain. Then in 1978, AGMA kicked in with the Dance Theatre Harlem and one of the changes they brought with the membership was there would be no work on any travel day. In other words, on a day when the company travelled to or from a venue, there was to be no ballet class or rehearsal.

This was the case when the company made their next stop in Mississippi. Having landed and then checked in to their hotel, Arthur Mitchell had to reluctantly abide by the union's ruling, so there were no classes or rehearsals until the following day. However, when the class was due to start at the theatre on that second day, Mitchell didn't show. One of the principle girl dancers, Lorraine, was also a ballet mistress, so she took the morning class. That was followed by a stage rehearsal, and still there was no sign of Arthur Mitchell and rumours began to spread concerning some unrest amongst the local community regarding the ballet company performing.

Halfway through that stage rehearsal, Mitchell finally appeared and immediately called a company meeting with an element of fear obvious in his eyes. He stood before everyone and quietly explained, "Due to severe unrest and protests from the Klu Klux Klan, tonight's performance has been cancelled."

There were gasps of astonishment from every person there. After all, the DTH had always performed in front of mixed audiences, both black and white people who enjoyed wholeheartedly what was always a magical evening's entertainment and nothing more than that.

"The Klan are protesting at the moment, outside the theatre and we've been advised to return to our hotel and wait there until further notice," Mitchell continued solemnly, "So I think it best to follow that advice and I'll see about re-arranging our flight out of here. Leave the theatre quietly, in two's or three's might be best."

The dancers did as Arthur Mitchell had requested and when Julie reached the street outside, she and the other dancers had to walk past a horde of people dressed in white gowns with pointed hats and masks bearing torn out scary eyeholes. It was terrifying for the young black dancers, having to listen to foul abuse and bullying threats thrown at them, as they made their way along the sidewalk towards where their hotel was located. But each of them held their heads up high and walked with straight backs, showing no sign of the terrifying fear churning away at their insides. They were proud, brave and courageous, unlike the miscreants hiding behind their pointed hoods, unaffected by the shame normal people would have shared by such a disgraceful exhibition.

But, this was Mississippi, which stood proud on its record for burning out, beating up and murdering innocent black people, men, women and children. And it seemed that, even after all the condemnation and protests from the rest of the civilised world, the Mississippi mountain of criminal racist filth, upon which these misguided skulkers stood with grinning and contorted faces on the very summit, remained unchallenged.

Throughout that night Arthur Mitchell earned a great deal of respect from his staff, continually speaking to every member of his company, trying to reassure them that he was doing all he could to get them out of this pathetic and abhorrent place, apologising for having ever accepted an engagement there in the first place. He showed genuine concern, acting like a father figure, embracing and doing his best to put an arm around his people during this traumatic time, in which they were so obviously suffering. Finally, after trying so hard to find the earliest flight out of this damned city, he got his company booked on an early morning flight back to New York.

There can be little doubt that when such wonderful and artistic talent is performed in public, as was always the case with DTH, much joy and knowledge can be gained by those privileged to observe such performances, except of course, for that minority who fear such social elements. Sadly, those are the few who remain happy to continue their lives in ignorance and in the case of the KKK, blatant criminality. However, that kind of person is without importance and unworthy of recognition from an educated and civilised world, therefore, once the company had left the illiterate blindness behind them, there was no place in their memory for what had happened, and only happiness and enlightenment awaited them in more civilised societies.

When they returned to New York, Julie was met by Joe, who was bursting at the seams to give her some wonderful news. During the time they had known each other, Julie had told her mother all about her new boyfriend, and in fact had furnished both of them with each other's telephone numbers. During the time Julie had been on tour, Joe had spoken to Doreen Felix who had confirmed that she and Julie's sister, Lucia would be visiting New York in the summer of that year, to make up for their disappointment at not having the chance to see Julie when she was supposed to have returned home at the end of her first twelve month contract. Of course, the girl from Ealing was overjoyed and now realising she would be staying in New York much longer than had been anticipated, decided to leave the Webster House for girls and look for other accommodation which didn't have its own small army of vigilantes with excessive boobs, although she had truly enjoyed their company.

One of the other girls at DTH, Sharon, was living in an apartment in 87th Street on the West Side and had just lost her roommate, which meant she had a spare room. When she offered it to Julie, it was like offering her pennies from Heaven. Julie was quick to move in and from the twenty fifth floor apartment, fell in love with the panoramic views it afforded her, of the city and over Central Park. Life in America was certainly moving upwards for the would-be starlet.

Chapter Twenty-Three

Family Reunion

The company landed right bang in the middle of a typical Californian heat wave, with just about everybody in shorts, vests or T shirts, including the dancers and technicians. Julie's first sighting of San Francisco was of a thriving city with people trying unsuccessfully not to rush about because of the high temperatures. It wasn't that much different from New York, apart from the steep gradients and trolley buses which seemed to dominate the centre of the famous metropolis.

One of the girls had arranged for Julie to stay with her parents who lived in the surrounding hills, overlooking the Golden Gate Bridge and she was allocated a room with spectacular views spanning the whole of Frisco's fascination. Thankfully, there was air conditioning in the theatre which made classes and rehearsals bearable.

Every morning, she looked down on a veil of mist that seemed to stretch the whole length of the city, totally covering the bridge with its cables reaching out towards the sky in ghostly fashion. It was indeed a far cry from the grey skies and falling rain synonymous with Ealing and St Louis. Then it happened, one morning, before even the earliest risers had shaken themselves from their slumber, Julie suddenly felt her room shaking. A couple of pictures dropped from the wall and the sound of items crashing to the floor elsewhere in the house, induced a feeling of terror as she opened her bedroom door. Here we go again, what the hell was happening? So far that year, the company hadn't been on tour without there being some kind of incident resulting in postponement. Would this be another of those freak episodes?

"Don't worry, this sort of thing happens all the time in Frisco," her friends parents told her, standing just outside her door, huddled together before explaining it was yet another earthquake, but only a small interruption, probably registering no more than a seven on the Richter Scale. Imagine the kind of panic just a 'seven on the Richter Scale' would have brought to London, or any other British city if it came to that. Well the quake lasted for just three minutes and items that hadn't been smashed, were put back in their rightful places, before normal service was resumed. At least that night's performance took place, ending with the usual appreciative acclaim, before the company flew out of 'Earthquake City' with some relief.

When Dance Theatre Harlem returned to New York, Julie's mind was busy once again, this time targeting ways in which she could climb another rung of the ladder to success and the only way up was achieving a position in the company as a soloist or principle ballerina. What was known as the cast list was left on a wall at the DTH studio every morning, instructing the dancers what roles they were to rehearse for that day. Some, including Julie, were always down for rehearsing in the corps de ballet, while others had different responsibilities, including the solo roles in which she had become ambitious to achieve. But how could she make the break through without asking Arthur Mitchell directly, which would have been the same as asking a vampire to go for a stroll in the sun.

The company structure of performers was a simple one, a replica of most other ballet companies. For members of the corps de ballet, there were two grades of pay, the lowest going to the novice dancer and a pay rise being awarded to the second year performer. Then as a soloist dancer, the pay was increased for a second cast dancer and went up even higher when a performer became what was known as a first cast dancer. It was all about climbing up those rungs of the ladder until you reached the very top, which only a few ever achieved, a Prima Ballerina. But, even though she was pre-occupied most of the time with thoughts of her mother's and sister's forthcoming visit, she remained determined to achieve.

Firstly, she needed a strategy, a plan to get noticed and force Mr. Mitchell to consider elevating Julie up the ranks. She became a frequent visitor to the studio where the soloist roles were being re-enacted and would stand in a corner, mimicking some of the dancers, putting on the kind of individual performances that would have attracted anybody's attention. She knew that eventually Mitchell would have to see her and take notice of the hint she was trying so hard to communicate. Of course she was openly flaunting her intentions, but there was no room for protocol or concordance in Julie's mind. She wanted promotion, knew she was good enough and was going to do her bloody upmost to get it.

It was one mid-morning when Julie was there as usual, having suddenly appeared in the soloists studio as if she'd fallen through the ceiling, floating around the studio floor with all the grace she could muster, at the same time watching closely the other dancers. The company director suddenly stopped what he was doing and called out, "Okay, Julie, that's enough, get yourself back to your own studio, where you should be rehearsing with the rest of the corps de ballet."

That slight admonishment didn't bother her particularly; she'd asked the unspoken question of the man and didn't really care what his thoughts were. If he had liked what he had seen he would do something about it, otherwise she would just continue in her present position. The main thing was, Arthur Mitchell was now aware that he had one hell of an ambitious girl on his hands. Whether he thought she was good enough for promotion was another thing entirely.

The following day, the cast list didn't include Julie's name in the corps de ballet, instead it was visible with the rest of the soloist dancers. She'd won her battle, achieved her short term ambition, but now there remained the small problem of having to prove herself. Only then, after dancing solo in front of a live audience would she be able to truly call herself a soloist ballerina.

By the time the summer of 1978 arrived, Julie was nearing the end of her first year with the Dance Theatre Harlem, but rather than preparing for a homeward trip, leaving her experiences and dreams behind, she was busy readying herself for a reunion with her beloved mother and sister, amongst New York's finest. Her mind was totally filled with exciting anticipation and just about every other emotion imaginable. The company were also winding down towards a six week close down, which was an annual event and fortuitously for Julie, couldn't have come at a better time, leaving her free to spend as much time as possible with her family visitors to the Big Apple.

Joe offered to accompany her to Kennedy Airport to meet Doreen and Lucia and the couple stood staring at the Arrivals Gate, like two kids yearning for an ice cream sundae that was beyond their reach. As the clock ticked away, the tension grew, bringing with it negative thoughts, such as, what if the plane had actually somersaulted down the runway or some other awful tragedy had happened. Flight passengers came and went, disappearing towards the many taxi ranks outside the main terminal. Julie couldn't take her eyes away from the monitoring screen, waiting patiently, shuffling her feet.

"Joe, what if ..."

"We're early, Julie, they'll be here soon enough."

The squeaking wheels of luggage trolleys momentarily distracted her and then the flight they were looking for came up as 'landed' and Julie's heart began to pulsate through her whole body. She smiled nervously as more people began to filter through the gate, pushing more of those damned squeaking trolleys. Then suddenly, and as if the film had stopped and one slide remained frozen in full view, there they were. Doreen Felix looking no different from when Julie had last seen her at Heathrow, dressed in a bright floral dress, looking as if she'd just stepped through the brightly coloured door of their home back in Ealing and showing no signs of having flown three thousand miles across the Atlantic. Lucia stood at her mother's side, also looking quite debonair in a tight figure-hugging skirt and cotton blouse, with a wide smile which added joy to the scene that presented itself to her sister.

Julie's throat tightened and the heavens opened up in her eyes.

"Julie," her mother cried out, holding both arms invitingly for her long lost daughter to seek refuge within.

Her daughter saw no one else, nothing more than the two women standing there before her. She rushed forward on jellified legs and threw herself into her mum's arms, crying, burying her face in a comforting shoulder, not ever wanting to let this wonderful woman go again.

"It's so good to see you, love." Mum's voice hadn't changed one iota either.

Then she turned to hug her sister, Lucia, and both girls cried tears of joy in unison. There were no words spoken, just their eyes meeting with mutual unspoken questions of how could life be so good, so kind; how could this reunion ever end. They all prayed it never would.

Finally, the tears eased and the initial joy subsided sufficiently for Julie to introduce Joe, whose extreme politeness and kind-looking face made an immediate impact on Doreen. A repeat performance of what Julie had experienced when she first landed in New York, then followed, pushing their heavy trolley with suitcases bulging full of English treats for the slim ballerina, towards the queues for the yellow cabs. Joe never hesitated in offering advice and directing his city's latest visitors through the human traffic with calmness and efficiency.

Julie hoped Sam would be there with his cab and even looked around, just in case he was about, but of course, that possibility was virtually an impossibility. But once inside some other driver's yellow cab, heading for the West Side, the chatter began amongst the three women.

"Julie, you look so thin," stated mum.

"You haven't picked up an American accent," commented her sister.

"How I've missed you both and you do look oh so well," declared Julie.

Both visitors paused to stare at the same Manhattan skyline Julie had feasted her eyes on when being comforted by Sam the Cabbie all those centuries ago. But this time, she sat back watching the pleasure in her mother and sister's eyes, after all, she was now a New Yorker. This was her Metropolis, her city, her home now and she told her mother just that.

Chapter Twenty-Four

Double Whammy

Both Doreen and Lucia were bewildered by the magnitude of New York, Julie's mother finding it difficult to accept that her youngest daughter had actually survived, living all alone in this concrete complexity of skyscrapers, fast food and noisy streets. During that six week summer break many of the dancers had left the city to travel home to various parts of the United States, some seeking casual employment just to get sufficient funds to see them through the annual break from DTH. Julie's friend Sharon, had vacated the apartment to visit her home town, Chicago, which left enough space to house Doreen and Lucia.

When they finally entered the apartment, Julie's mum looked out across the city and gasped, "Gosh, Julie, it's so high up here." The other two girls laughed and Julie wondered what her mother's reaction would be one hundred floors up in one of the World Trade Towers. There was no doubting how impressed both visitors were by Julie's home in the sky, surrounded by such a vast urban landscape.

The following few days were filled with more excitement than Julie had ever experienced before, visiting Joe's rented summer home on Fire Island and slumming it on a nearby beach which reminded both Julie and Lucia of those short holidays at the seaside with mum and dad. At first they struggled a little with the heat, but that was soon forgotten once they'd reached Fire Island, getting there by train and then boat. It was like a small paradise isle, with wonderful white sanded beaches and Joe's house was somewhat unique in that the shape was more like a kite than an orthodox building. It was all so magical and impressive.

As the English visitors stay was only to last for a couple of weeks, Julie did her utmost to pack as much as possible into their visit. She also threw a party, inviting some of the DTH dancers who had remained in New York, wanting so badly to introduce her mother and sister to her work colleagues and friends.

They were taken to the Empire State Building, Central Park, the Rockefeller Centre, St Patrick's Cathedral, which would never be the same again for Julie, having stood in front of the altar with her mum at her side, and of course the World Trade Centres, which made Doreen just a little dizzy. But the tours were full of fun, chatter and exhilaration, all three ladies being totally exhausted come each nightfall.

The two week stay went by far too quickly and sadness began to creep into Julie as the day for her mother and sister's departure loomed nearer. If only they could have stayed longer, or perhaps forever. But alas, in similar fashion to how Julie had walked to that plane at Heathrow twelve months previously, it was her turn to stand and wave as her mum and sister walked away, frequently turning to wave back and throw as many kisses to her as they could. Finally they both disappeared from sight, to return to another world, their world, which Julie had once been a major part of. The tears had returned and her throat clamped up like she had some kind of infection.

For a time she just stood there, frozen to the spot, keeping her eyes transfixed on the last place she'd actually seen her wonderful mother and sister. The lost child had returned, full of emptiness and loneliness, before turning to anger and bitterness which flowed through her sleek body like a raging torrent seeking the edge of a cliff. But she had developed control as she had matured and all of the ups and downs during that previous twelve months had left her a much harder person, more capable of dealing with adversity and by far, a much stronger lady.

"Come on, Julie, time to go," advised Joe, placing a comforting arm around her waist. It was time to return to the hustle and bustle of the city, the enormous population made up of people with whom she could now associate, New Yorkers, flyers, dreamers, scoundrels and those people who were just living out their ambitions, all bonded together by the fact they were Americans and proud to be so.

Then came a double whammy that again added to the downside of Julie's very being. By the time the new rehearsal period began at DTH, the air was full of excitement and enthusiasm, with everybody returning refreshed from their summer break and biting at the bit to get working again. Julie had settled nicely in Sharon's apartment, but then found her flat mate appearing to become a little distant, conversing curtly, almost shyly, but without any hostility in her voice. She was just at times, aloof, something the English girl hadn't experienced before with Sharon.

She tried to work out the cause of this change in her friend's character. Had Julie done something to upset her? She'd spent hours after her mum and sister had left, keeping the apartment clean and tidy, so that couldn't be the reason. But as those few initial return to work days went by, the distance between the two girls began to increase. Finally, Julie decided it had to be connected to some kind of gulf that existed between English and American personalities, although she had no idea what that could be, so her decision was made. She would confront Sharon face to face in an attempt to clear the air.

When challenged with Julie's question as to what had gone wrong in their relationship, Sharon answered in a whisper, but with honesty.

"I don't know how to tell you this, Julie, but I've started seeing Joe."

"My Joe?"

Sharon just nodded, her eyes dropping to the floor.

The bomb exploded inside Julie's head and all the joyful stars she retained in her mind disappeared. So that was it. Julie couldn't believe the words just thrown at her. Joe, her Joe, had been two timing her and later confirmed as much when she confronted him with the allegation. The polite-speaking, humble and kind Joe had broken her heart and for the first time, Julie had been stroked with failure and deceit. But, she accepted these things happen in life and although she had loved this boy from Brooklyn so very much, which made the break up harder to take, there was nothing she could do, other than pack her bags and move out. God knows how many times she cursed Sharon and Joe for having let her down so badly, but life just had to go on and the pain she felt was banished to that shelf in the back of her mind reserved only for bad memories.

It didn't take her long to find another apartment in her favourite New York location, Greenwich, and after moving in with two other girls who were members of the company, Julie launched herself into her work, filling every moment she had with dance routines, rehearsing and company classes. She quickly discovered that Pilates had become an excellent tool for strengthening dancers' bodies, being particularly effective with individual performers who sustained injury.

Designed during the first half of the twentieth century by a German physical-culturist, Joseph Pilates, it was a system of exercises intended to strengthen both the human mind and body in the belief that mental and physical health are interrelated. The system demands constant intensive concentration and focus, underlining the fact that the way in which the exercises are carried out is far more important than the exercises themselves.

Julie studied Pilates with Cathy Grant, one of the more experienced and capable teachers in New York who had a studio on Fifth Avenue, where Julie would attend before making the early morning class at Dance Theatre Harlem. At first, Cathy Grant's teaching was hard, even harder than Arthur Mitchell's approach, but Julie quickly began to feel the benefits of the private lessons. Her strength increased dramatically, resulting in her ballet technique becoming more enhanced, assisting her towards her goal to become a soloist. Thank you, oh thank you, Miss Grant.

Shortly after restarting at the dance studio in Harlem, a history making incident took place, not because of Julie's strengthened agility, but it was more to do with Arthur Mitchell employing for the first time, a white male dancer to perform with the Dance Theatre Harlem. Joe Cipolla, another true American of Italian descent, was good, in fact brilliant as a performer, but he was surprisingly subjected to a great deal of persecution from the other staff. In fact, there the kind of upheaval that swept through the company like an uncontrolled bush fire, similar to what the company had experienced in Mississippi, only in reverse.

DTH had been built on the philosophy that it was an institution for black dancers only, its very soul generating black culture and tremendous popularity from those who loved the Afro-American accents so prominent in the company's performances. But Mitchell was no fool, and having been on top of his game for so long, knew true talent when it hit him in the face. He had recognised that Cipolla possessed all the signs and indications of being not just a good ballet dancer, but a brilliant one, perhaps one day, the greatest of them all.

Julie sympathised with the new addition, relating his situation with some of what she'd experienced, particularly in England, so decided to take the bewildered young man under her wing, teaching, advising, supporting and reassuring the guy that all would be well, eventually. She shared her rigorous Pilates exercises, demonstrating to the newcomer, the same methods she had learned under the tuition of Cathy Grant. Under her direction, Joe Cipolla soon settled and in time became accepted by the rest as just another dancer, as if he was one of their own, dancing as if he was one of their own.

Soon, the Autumn touring schedule began and both Julie and her new found Joe, became closer until a relationship developed between them. The winds of change were continuous in her young life and the Julie of old, the same girl who had left the shores of her own country more than a year before, had disappeared for good.

Chapter Twenty-Five

Michael Jackson

By the Spring of 1980 Julie and Joe Cipolla were virtually living together, sharing a room and constantly exchanging ideas and philosophy about their chosen profession, living in each other's pockets and understanding their mutual concerns about the day to day routines of life in The Ballet industry. Such cross fertilisation was beneficial to both and they had each earned the total respect for their individual talents from the rest of the company.

Julie's dream of one day being a professional ballet dancer first began when she was a small school girl, being watched closely and encouraged by an enthusiastic teacher, Miss Bray, at Northfields Secondary Modern School. She had progressed with Joyce Butler's School of Dance, leaping across uneven floorboards in St Paul's Church Hall in Ealing, before opening doors after a three year course at Angela Ellis's Ballet Rambert. When finally being taken into the Dance Theatre Harlem under the guiding hand of Arthur Mitchell, not once during those preceding years of study and practice had she ever contemplated or believed in becoming legendary or even celebrated as a dancer. But that might have all changed when in the Spring of 1980 DTH travelled to Pasadena, California for an unusual engagement.

After returning to the California sun, both Julie and her new found Joe went sight-seeing together whenever an opportunity came their way, visiting the famous Sunset Boulevard and Hollywood Hills, dominated by arguably the most photographed and filmed 'street sign' in the district, the famous boarding with the legend Hollywood printed in huge letters. It was beneath that sign, gazing down at the small town and clusters of movie stars residences, that Julie suddenly felt she must have been the luckiest young woman alive.

When they returned to the theatre for rehearsals the following day, they were greeted by the other dancers who told them about rumours that none other than one of the greatest entertainers of all time, Michael Jackson, was making arrangements to watch their matinee performance. Of course everyone was thrilled by the news, especially Julie as it was to be her debut as a second cast soloist performing Adagietto Number Five.

The tension and anticipation amongst the DTH performers went sky high, the rumours being confirmed when the security around the theatre was suddenly increased by men in black suits and dark shades, wandering freely around the immediate vicinity, wearing ear pieces and seemingly talking to their wrist watches. It was as if President Carter himself was about to land and the 'all in black' contingency was his advance guard.

As was her usual habit, Julie went up on stage behind the closed curtain for early practice with other members, but the sounds they heard from the paying customers entering the auditorium were different. All the performers could hear were screams of, "Michael, we love you."

Mitchell's people looked across at each other, grinning, nodding and already becoming absorbed in whatever was going down on the other side of the curtain. One of the youngest dancers, Veronique, a small talented girl who Arthur Mitchell had only recently recruited off the streets of Harlem, turned her head towards one of the wings.

"Look, Julie," the talented youngster quietly said.

They all followed Veronique's eyes to where a number of black suits were quietly conversing, giving out various directions, addressing other invisible people and all confirming that somebody special was about to appear. And he did so. Similar to a phantom or other apparition suddenly moving out of the backstage shadows, into the subdued lighting on stage, Jackson, the King of Pop briefly appeared, surrounded by bodyguards, but sufficiently visible for all the DTH dancers to see him clearly.

Then, as quickly as he had emerged he disappeared again, his minders quickly shuffling him from backstage towards one of the most prominent boxes in the theatre. Well, at least Michael Jackson had succeeded in usurping Julie's debut performance and she was determined to get her own back, by dancing in a way even the great pop idol would find irresistible. When the show began, she danced as if her life depended on it, as though it was to be her first and final showcase in public, but no one saw her, except the only person in the audience who wasn't staring at himself.

"We love you Michael" continued to echo from the sell-out crowd, bouncing off the walls of every room inside the theatre. Of course Julie was annoyed by the disturbance, until she realised that the super star was actually there to watch her dance. So, with the same ever present grace and agility she had now become accustomed to displaying, she danced out her role with such ease of movement, and both daring and courage added to her poise and unbelievable control. The screaming subsided and heads turned towards the graceful black ballet dancer, displaying her talents in such a magical and entertaining manner. A star sat in one of the boxes, but another star occupied the stage, enjoying her ability to mesmerise the audience.

Upon completion of the ballet, the same screams went up again, "Michael we love you," but not after every person in that auditorium had given Julie and the rest of the company a robust standing ovation. Just wait until she had a chance to tell her mum all about this one.

After the curtain fell for the third time, all of the dancers were asked to remain on stage to meet the biggest icon in the history of pop music, plus his dark glasses and professionally applied make-up. He walked slowly across the stage and stood before them, appearing to be more nervous meeting them individually, as they did of shaking hands with him. Julie was the last of them to face Michael Jackson and he spoke with a soft voice, congratulating her on a wonderful and magical performance. Grasping both gloved hands together, he quietly asked for her name and where she came from and she nervously told him.

"I have truly enjoyed the performance, Julie," he declared, "And want all of you to appear in a new film I want to make about your English Peter Pan."

Julie was flabbergasted at the suggestion that not just herself, but the whole of DTH might just possibly become household names. She smiled and told Jackson, "I'm sure Mr. Mitchell and all of us would be honoured to work with you, sir."

He stepped back a pace and smiled back at her.

"Thank you, Julie and God Bless you."

After Michael Jackson had left, together with his entourage and the rest of the dancers, Julie remained, standing alone on the very spot which she had occupied since conversing with the main man. Wow, if only it happened. No matter how great a person can be, artistically, or how famous they become, we are all human beings who enter this world with nothing and leave it with the same. That was how that young super star's presence had influenced her way of thinking. Yes, we are all human beings and its life's experiences that moulds us into the kind of people we become. She would never forget who she was and where she had come from and Julie had to later admit, she had never met a more humble and dignified man in her life, before that meeting with Michael Jackson.

The decline of the Jackson Empire has been well documented, explaining the various reasons why it became quite obvious there would never be sufficient funds raised to make the kind of film, lodged inside Michael's mind and which is now confined to history. And so it was, the idea of making a Peter Pan the Movie never came to fruition.

But if meeting and conversing with Michael Jackson was the highlight of her career thus far, one of the lowest points she ever experienced came shortly after that meeting in Pasadena. The girl from Harlem, Veronique, had left the theatre with another of the male dancers who had rented a car for the season. The excited couple had chosen to drive down Sunset Boulevard, when the car suddenly veered off the highway, hitting one of the overhead street lamps. The street furniture collapsed, breaking in two before the top half came crashing down, falling directly on top of the young girl who was almost cut in two. Veronique died instantly and was never to dance again.

She had been an orphan, leaving behind no one to attend her funeral, so every member of the company made it, standing in silence with heads bowed to pay their respects to this wonderfully talented ballet dancer, who had so much to offer the world of entertainment. It was indeed a sad loss and Veronique would be missed by all of those gifted friends she had met up with during her short stay with the Dance Theatre Harlem.

The next tour for DTH that year was to Washington DC and after landing there, the company made their way to the hotel which had been booked for the duration. As with most engagements in the American cities, the dancers got used to people just stopping to stare at them. That didn't bother them, though; they all understood why others would be inquisitive at the sight of a large group of extremely attractive, athletic looking young black people, who all resembled professional models. Of course, the crew that always accompanied them looked much different, more like your average person, looking well out of place amongst the dancers. They included that ancient lady, Miss Winn and then there was the co-director, Karl Shook with his white hair and creased face. The company manager was a very tall and thin man who also looked out of place when rubbing shoulders with the much younger professionals.

When they reached their Washington hotel, it was time to rest, in accordance with union rules that stipulated no work on a travel day, so some of the company decided to take a short trip around the country's capital, intent on seeing what all the fuss had been about concerning a dormant nearby volcano, Mount St Helens. Some people staying in the same hotel had mentioned the landmark was well worth seeing. They'd also mentioned something about the volcano beginning to rumble, but that remark fell on deaf ears amongst the dancers who were still mindful of having recently met their hero back in Pasadena. In addition to that, this was also the USA's seat of power where they were about to perform. The small party from DTH made it, almost, before being stopped from going further and being told it might not be all that safe at the present time. Everyone laughed, even when they were told there were scientists in the region watching the rumbling mountain closely. The following morning left them all in shock, something they didn't need after the recent loss of their friend, Veronique.

Chapter Twenty-Six

Mount St Helens

At exactly 8.32 a.m. the following morning, on the 18 May 1980 while the company of the Dance Theatre Harlem were breakfasting at their Washington hotel, there was a tremendous explosion which shook the whole building so badly, most people inside were certain the building would never survive the shock waves. Residents screamed and ran to the terraces, leaving plates of food and personal belongings at the tables they had just vacated.

Julie stood with some of the other dancers, watching through a floor to ceiling open window as Mount St. Helens erupted, throwing out a large twelve mile high mushroom similar to a black cloud of vengeance, up into the Washington sky. No one spoke a word, everyone just stood still, watching in shock as the volcano continued to spew out its clouds of ash, turning what had been a cloudless blue sky into a dark eclipse hovering over the entire city. The north face of the mountain was destroyed, which thankfully, had been on the opposite side to where

DTH's hotel was located, otherwise the casualty list might well have been a lot more than the fifty seven people killed as a result of the eruption. It was and still is the worst volcanic disaster in American history.

The eruption lasted for another nine hours, street lights automatically switching on over an area of three hundred miles, even though it was in the middle of the day, but as a result of the darkness engulfing the streets and countryside surrounding the capital. Records show two hundred and fifty homes were destroyed, together with forty seven bridges, fifteen miles of railway and one hundred and eighty five miles of highway. More than a thousand feet was lopped off Mount St Helen's summit during the episode.

Nature's calamitous disaster brought about the obvious cancellation of the Dance Theatre Harlem's engagement, although that was the last thing on everyone's mind. After the skies began to finally clear, everywhere was covered in ash, and in true American capitalistic style, people were soon back on the streets, sweeping up and collecting samples of ash in whatever small glass phials they could find, to sell later to tourists at a buck a piece.

During the short time in which Julie had been touring with DTH she had experienced a black out which crippled New York for the first time, the heaviest snowfall in the city's history, which had the same effect, a fierce electrical storm while dining out on the one hundredth floor of the World Trade Centre, floods in St Louis, an earthquake in San Francisco and a face to face confrontation with the Klu Klux Klan in Mississippi. And now America's worst ever volcanic eruption in Washington. Yet, all the girl ever wanted to do was dance in The Ballet. It was just unbelievable that the girl's period spent in this vast country, had witnessed so many record breaking disasters. At one stage, she even thought about wearing a St Christopher around her neck.

There were two loves now in Julie's life, The Ballet and Joe Cipolla and time seemed to fly past, the girl with the English accent unable to slow things down. Everything was moving like a Cheetah showing off its fleetness of movement across an open plain. As each performance was successfully completed, Arthur Mitchell gave Julie more important roles to dance, although he never gave her the chance to dance with Joe as her partner.

"For the pair of you to dance a pas de deux, would be like a wife teaching her husband how to drive, a recipe for disaster," he once told her. Then the day eventually arrived that sent Julie's heart pumping and her mind into orbit. The day she had dreamed of and wished for since leaving her roots behind in Ealing. Dance Theatre Harlem had been booked for a season at the Sadler's Wells Theatre in London.

It wouldn't be the first time the company had set foot on English soil; of course, they had been performing there when Julie auditioned, before being offered a contract. But, it would be the first time they would be dancing before a British audience, with Julie amongst their numbers. She became dizzy, trying to picture the scenes that lay before her, dancing lead with a world-renowned and acclaimed company in a theatre just up the road from where her parents lived. The first thing she did was to invite her friend who had allowed her to stay with her parents in earthquake chastened San Francisco, to stay in her humble abode beyond her father's brightly painted front door. At least there wouldn't be much danger of a performance being cancelled as a result of anti-black protesters or some major disaster performed by Mother Nature. In addition, her new found love, Joe Mark II would also be with her and it would be an opportunity for Julie to act as a tour guide around her own city. She was already making a list of London's places of interest to visit.

After the plane landed at Heathrow, the first moment of pride for the local girl came when the rest of the company had to pass through the American passport exit, while Julie nonchalantly strolled through the UK section. When they all made the arrivals terminal as one complete group, there stood her mother and father, waiting patiently, smiling and waving, as she did the same to them, noting there were no squeaking trolleys around on this occasion.

It had been a long time since Julie last set eyes on her father and suddenly she realised just how much she'd missed the old Hoover factory foreman. They hugged each other warmly and for the first and only time in her life, she noticed his eyes had turned watery.

"Dad," she said, "Don't cry."

"I'm not crying, girl," he answered back, almost croaking before turning his head away.

When Patrick met Arthur Mitchell, he acted as if he'd known the man for years, grasping his hand firmly and confirming, "I've always been on the side of the old USA you know."

The initial introduction to Joe Cipolla was somewhat different, in that Patrick looked a little confused, acting like a fiddler having been asked to play a harmonica, obviously wondering just which Joe this was standing in front of him with a broad Yankee smile. But, once the two gents had broken the ice there was only one way, and that was up, with both Julie's father and boyfriend getting along like a house on fire.

On the way to the family home in Ealing, after leaving the rest of the company to find their hotel, the one amazing thing Julie noticed was how small everything looked. There were no six lane highways or high rise skyscrapers adorning the views around them, no traffic cop constantly blowing his whistle or cabbies competing for the biggest foul mouth of the year. Having been absent for two or three years, everything seemed to be so quaint and most surprising of all was that people didn't shout or even look at you as though you were some kind of escaped specimen. When the small group finally arrived at the Felix homestead she noticed her father had painted the front door, yet another different bright colour from the one she remembered.

It didn't take long though for her faculties to return to those days of childhood, as a thousand things triggered various memories, such as the front gate squeaking, her mother's roses in full bloom with heads bowing in honour of the lost girl's return to the Kingdom. What was different was Patrick's attitude towards Julie. She was no longer his youngest daughter, but an American visitor, accompanied by American friends, entitled to receive his adoration and high regard for visitors from the country he had always admired. He even opened the door for Julie and Joe whenever they left or returned to the house, like a true gentleman, obviously overawed just a little by Joe's New York accent. Her parents had saved up enough money so they could impress their American visitors and make their stay as special as possible.

During that first evening, all five talked and talked some more about the dancers exciting life in the States and about everything that had happened to them on tour, with Patrick sitting in his favourite armchair listening intently, which was another first as far as Julie was concerned. Julie's friend remained humble throughout the verbal exchanges, as did Joe, while Doreen Felix, in between saying a few words, shuffled to and fro from the small kitchen, furnishing them all with a constant run of cups of tea.

The following day was just like any normal working day for the company, ballet class followed by rehearsals. Julie entered the theatre feeling quite proud at having successfully directed and ushered her two colleagues around the London Underground and through the crowded and narrow streets of England's capital city. The procedures when arriving at the theatre were exactly the same as always, sign in, check the cast list and note the dressing room number. Having completed those few initial chores, one of the theatre staff called to Julie, as she was about to make her way to her nominated dressing room. She was informed that there was a message for her in one of the stage door pigeon holes.

Curiously, she read the message which clearly stated that a national newspaper wanted to talk to her about a forthcoming article and that the BBC were requesting an interview with her, together with the England black cricketer, Basil D'Oliviera. Perhaps attitudes were finally changing in favour of black people, in this land of Robin Hood, green meadows and oak trees?

Julie had been dancing solo now for some time and found herself in the soloists dressing room with her black box full to the brim. She was aware that so many old friends and her parents were going to attend that opening night and everything had to be just right, so she took her time laying out the required items taken from inside the box. In other words, she carefully placed each component part of her machinery in orderly fashion, rather than just throw them down, as was her usual practice.

That night's performance was a milestone in Julie's long and hard working journey, her greatest ambition was about to be realised, to dance in front of a British audience as the first black ballerina to do so. A swan could never have glided across a lake more beautifully than she did. An eagle couldn't have soared upwards in the sky as magnificently as she did and no phantom on earth could have been more transparent as she was throughout that performance. Julie swayed the watching audience, triggering their appreciative senses with dream-like movements, which flowed like a slow running crystal clear river, other dancers adding effect like gnats skimming the surface. People gasped but remained silent in admiration of this wonderful and gifted dancer, whose feathery lightness kept them entranced like moths to a headlight beam.

At the end of the performance, there was that usual silent pause, when the audience wished for the magnificent display of true artistry to continue, when they experience an overwhelming need to remain in their seats, wishing for those commanding the stage never to leave.

Then came the applause and not one person remained seated when the hands clapped and the verbal plaudits filled the auditorium. In fact, they roared their approval and Julie embraced every cheer and acknowledgement. This was her night, the pinnacle of all she had achieved, the final accomplishment resulting from all the obstacles encountered since being a child living and dreaming in the backstreets of Ealing, London.

There were many firsts that night, following her unbelievable solo performance, Arthur Mitchell commented on how pleased he was and Patrick Felix appeared backstage with his arms outstretched and his face full of pride for his 'American' daughter. Two of her friends from another long ago era, Linda and David, also made it backstage, but could only stand there, speechless, shaking their heads in disbelief. They would later circulate to others the news of this miracle worker, this little black girl from Great Britain and what she had developed into. But the most amazing thing that happened on that night of glory, was her father taking them all out to celebrate at his favourite Chinese restaurant, and paying the bill, which Julie knew he couldn't really afford.

"I do love you, Dad," she kept whispering to herself.

The theatre, like all others in England, was closed every Sunday and that gave the small group of the Felix family and friends, an opportunity to go sightseeing, Julie giving a running commentary for Joe's benefit, as they passed by the Tower of London, Buckingham Palace, St Paul's Cathedral and many other favourites of the people. All during that day Joe and Patrick remained close, sharing a mutual admiration for each other, which lasted until they finally returned home as dusk was approaching.

As they entered the small house, Joe asked Patrick if he could look at some of the small garden at the back of the house and of course, Mr. Felix obliged the young American. It was then that the biggest surprise of the tour was thrust out of a hat without warning. Joe asked Patrick for Julie's hand in marriage. Well there was no revolving door, as Patrick had experienced with his own father in law, no flat rejection, instead his face lit up and he almost fell over with the excited joy he felt.

This wasn't really Julie's father giving a speech, was it? Patrick stood with a glass of spirit in one hand, after ensuring his small audience each had the same and began to drawl out his feelings straight from his heart.

"We are all very proud of our daughter, Julie, who has worked hard to make sure our money was well spent when we sent her off to find her destiny in New York. Let no man think we ever doubted our girl's potential."

Everyone smiled, except Julie who was still in shock.

"And I want you all to know, we are proud to know how famous she has become, especially now she is living in America and what's more, is about to be married to another American, Joe here, who I know is a fine upstanding man. I congratulate and salute them both."

That was it. Patrick had got everything off his chest and could now walk tall around the streets of Ealing telling everybody he met, about his famous American daughter. So, Julie had never seen this side of her father's character before, had never knew one existed, but she was happy and would never look at Patrick with the same eyes ever again. She threw a quick glance across at her fiancé and Joe just smiled back and winked an eye.

Chapter Twenty Seven

A Disastrous Blip

When the season finally ended at the Sadler's Wells Theatre, the company had their usual six week summer break and the recently engaged couple of young lovers decided to stay on in England. That was one hell of a period in Julie's life, well spent in sheer enjoyment of each other's company and the multitude of sights and locations they visited, with Julie always leading the way. But then, as with all good things, it had to end and a return to the States to join up with the other dancers was inevitable.

By the time that unwelcome departure came around, Julie had once again got used to having her mother at her side, and when the small family party arrived yet again at Heathrow Airport, she experienced yet more heartache. At least both mother and daughter had managed to add more wonderful recollections of happy times together in their existing memory banks.

The Dance Theatre Harlem was about to embark on a major touring schedule, taking in Hong Kong and Australia, and there was one hell of a lot of rehearsing to get through, leaving little time to earnestly get back into physical shape following the summer break. So it came to be, back breaking exercises and practice became the order of each day with Arthur Mitchell in the driving seat, brandishing a sharp tongue for any defaulters. The work, eat and sleep umbrella beneath which the dancers lived their lives for the first few days following their return, left many if not all of them totally exhausted and moving about like immigrants from someone else's dream.

It was late one evening when Julie returned home, walking as if every muscle had stopped working and her whole body was craving for rest and then some. Not wanting to hang about for too long, she decided to cook up some pasta, a quick and easy meal to sustain her until the following day.

Was it because of the sheer exhaustion that was dominating her mind and body, or just fate? She would never know. The ballerina's grasp on the handle of a pan of boiling hot water slipped and the biggest threat to her career so far, was the result. The water and pasta smothered her foot, soaking into a woollen sock which caused the heat to stick to her skin. Julie screamed in agony, and collapsed to the floor, her sub-conscious mind already ringing the alarm bells, already knowing the likely consequences.

Joe, who was in the next room, responded immediately and lifted Julie up before hastily carrying her across to a running tap of cold water, under which he held her foot; but alas, it was too late. Julie went into shock and began to convulse, her body shaking as if she was the recipient of some kind of fit. Again Joe reacted in the right way and managed to pack her injured foot with ice, before hoisting her up over his shoulder and without hesitation, running from the apartment, carrying her along the sidewalks to the nearby Accident and Emergency Department at Mount Sinai Hospital.

Before the doctors in attendance would even look at Julie's injury, they asked how she was going to pay for medical treatment, something that was completely alien and immoral to her. Had she got an Insurance Company to cover the expenses? If so, what was the name of the company and the name of the medical package meant to support her in cases of medical emergency. There was no health care system in the States, no NHS to tap into and hard cash was the only thing that would prevent you from losing a leg.

At that time, both Julie and Joe had just come back from an unpaid six week summer break and had little enough money between them. On top of that, just to have the privilege of seeing a nurse unroll a bandage cost hundreds of dollars, so that was the problem confronting them.

Julie began to pass out with the pain inflicted and the last thing on her mind was how the hell she going to pay for any treatment. The unpleasant trauma was also magnified by the number of druggies, stab victims and other poor penniless souls that were so prominent in A and E.

Joe begged for some help and finally, she got to see a doctor who decided to actively participate in helping this badly injured young lady out. The medic removed the woollen sock and stared down at the stricken foot for quite some time, before announcing the flesh had been completely scolded off down to the bone. He was also worried that various nerve endings could have been damaged and made his patient aware of his assessment.

That diagnosis filled Julie's eyes with terror and Joe's with utmost sympathy, both knowing what such a severe injury would mean. Her foot was quickly covered in a thick ointment and she was given heavy pain killers before being sent home, and after being told she mustn't walk and certainly not dance for a minimum of six weeks. The news was agonising, more so than the four hundred dollars she had to put up front there and then.

Having been told to return the following morning, Julie managed to hobble out, with some support from Joe and with only the thought of having her career, her life, ended in such a disastrous way. Yet, even before they'd got back to their apartment, the girl's resilience was beginning to surface. If she finished up with a club foot, somehow she would overcome whatever impediment was thrown at her. She knew it wasn't going to be a walk in the park, but by God she would dance again, even if she had to go through it all again on stilts. There was no way the lady was going to collapse under the strain placed on her by this career threatening accident, she would never give up, even if her best shot failed, she would bounce right back.

She told Arthur Mitchell that she intended to come through what she regarded as a blip and nothing more and although at first he seemed doubtful, he knew his girl and was well aware of the strength within her. So much so, he gave her confirmation of his belief by agreeing to keep paying Julie during the time it took her to recover. So it was, Julie went to work on that injured foot, driven by a strong belief that the impossible was possible.

The doctors had told her the damage sustained was so bad she might need a skin graft, taken from her groin, which for a ballet dancer, would have been more of a disaster than the injury to her foot. Julie declined to go down that route and with a lot of help from Joe, got down to the business of cleansing the weeping wound and redressing it three times a day. Where serious burns are involved, the blood must not be allowed to access the injured area and keeping the wound scrupulously clean was essential. It was like finding a new religion, continuing to follow the doctors instructions to the letter every day, spending the next six weeks doing absolutely nothing, except watch as her leg muscles began to waste away and allowing her body to deteriorate gradually. The six weeks felt like six years but by God, there was no way she was going to miss the Hong Kong and Australia tour.

Joe carried on working and reporting back to Julie any news he got from DTH, including her roles having been taken over by other dancers. She was living her worst nightmare, but continued to keep her leg elevated every night and day, fighting hard against the clouds of depression that were beginning to circle like vultures ready to sweep down and start picking at her bones. This particular death sentence that threatened her whole life's work and ambitions was never going to win and she held herself in check throughout that dark period of her life, constantly moving her mind in and out of black thoughts. She had to remain positive, she was positive and nothing on earth was going to derail her from her objective.

After that initial six week period of virtual isolation and nursing, Julie finally returned to work, only to find she had lost that much muscle tone and strength, there was no time to spare. This young lady who had come so far and achieved so much, was very much like a stranger in a faraway land, having to accept that everyone else had learned so much in her absence. The fact that her name was missing from the cast list, for obvious reasons, only added to her dilemma and for about a week, all she did, in between light exercises on the barre, was wallow in self-pity.

Then, one late evening, as she was hobbling through the front door of DTH's studio, down onto the street, she bumped into a friendly face, that of old Sam, who had first introduced Julie to New York. He was sitting inside his yellow cab and smiled through an open window.

"Hey, Julie," he shouted out in his best New York accent, "How's it going with you?"

She stopped and related her story of grief, missing out the bit about the medical expenses, which he'd know about anyway.

Sam glanced down at her heavily bandaged foot and said, "That sure does look like some kind of serious thing there, lady, but you know something, always remember, Julie, any problem can be made to disappear if you will it to, so you mustn't give up. Dig deep on all you have experienced in your life and show the world how much courage you have within you. Fight for what you want and then fight some more and you'll get there girl." Some New York cabbie this feller was.

But then, just as Julie was about to ask if he'd seen her inside St Patrick's Cathedral, he slowly drove away, disappearing into the greyness of dusk. She knew there and then, there was something special about that old man, some sort of gift he had to make her feel better, stronger and at one with the rest of the world. She suddenly felt as if a load of worry and anxiety had just been lifted from her shoulders. If it was possible to bottle up old Sam's demeanour and wisdom and carry it about with her, how much better her life would be. But then she realised, she'd just done exactly that, and she felt her physical strength and will power increasing, flowing through her like some kind of magic star dust spreading nothing but good news. There was no way now, Julie wouldn't be going on tour with the company.

The following day saw Julie at the dance studio before anyone else, beginning the most rigorous routine she had ever done before in her life. She went to Pilates several times a week, beginning at eight every morning, before making the studio to work on her own exercises. Even when the company was in full rehearsals, she would be present, intending to show Mr. Mitchell that she was back in full force, patiently waiting for the day when her name would once again appear on the cast list as a soloist. The self-torture was no stranger to her, often remembering those days at Rambert when she thought her whole body was about to explode. Oh yes, she'd been down this road before, even if it had been for different reasons and there would be no letting up this time either.

Days passed by, weeks took their toll, but slowly Julie's recovery was complete and she was ready. Julie Felix was back and by God, the miracle that had brought about her return would be repaid in full. So, there it was in front of her. She wanted to take it off the wall and get it framed. Julie's name was back on the cast list and above all, she had been given her rightful position in the company as a soloist ballet dancer. Thank you, Joe, thank you, Mr. Mitchell and a special thanks to old Sam the cabbie.

Chapter Twenty-Eight

Meeting the President

During the company's tour of Hong Kong, there was one occasion when Julie noticed a fairly long queue winding itself around one of the harbours, mostly made up of young folk and heading for a National Museum. It was impossible to count the number of heads in that queue but the figure must have run into hundreds. When she asked someone about the reason why so many of Hong Kong's youth were happily waiting their turn to enter the museum, she was told a rare collection of Egyptian relics was on display.

She couldn't believe the amount of widespread interest in an event that wasn't connected with the appearance of a pop idol or banned 'X' rated film, but rather, a load of Egyptian relics. That kind of fanaticism and high level enthusiasm in artistic culture and historical interest was carried over to each of DTH's performances, with the audiences going wild with excitement, during and after each show.

The whole company made more friends during that excursion to such a small location on the Eastern map than they had ever done before on any of their many tours. In fact all were sad and disappointed to leave, as they boarded the plane for Australia.

After landing in Sydney, they were escorted to their hotel in a district known as Kings Cross, which gave Julie an amazing sensation of being closer to home. If only her parents small home with the brightly coloured door was just a couple of miles down the road. But talk about it being a small world, as soon as Julie entered the hotel where they were all staying, she was given a message left there by an old friend from Rambert. Jenny had qualified through the Dance School but had given up dancing to get married and raise a family in Sydney and had obviously heard about her old friend's success with Dance Theatre Harlem.

The two young ladies arranged to meet and hugged each other with all the warmth and admiration one would expect to see when two old friends met up for the first time in years, on the opposite side of the world to where they had last set eyes on one another. There was a mountain of things to talk about and Jenny took Julie on a boat trip around Sydney Harbour, pointing out the magnificent Sydney Opera House.

"Do you remember when Miss Ellis…"

"Oh yes, and what about when…"

Both girls chatted nonstop until the sun finally went down, leaving

Julie thrilled at having met her old friend. It was indeed a very small world.

After fulfilling their engagements in Sydney, the next stop for the company was Melbourne where another pleasant surprise awaited the company. Even before their first rehearsal, they were all invited for lunch at a large house owned by the film star, Vincent Price. There were those amongst the group that wondered whether there would be bats flying about with bunches of garlic nailed to every door. But, they may have been disappointed because everything was to the contrary and they found the fangless star to be extremely charming and approachable. They all sat down to enjoy a buffet lunch with Mr. Price answering a multitude of questions thrown at him about his life in Hollywood. It was like visiting a next door neighbour - that was if you also lived in a mansion. There unusual lunch break fleetingly passed by and when the time came to leave, they were only allowed to do so, after photographs had been taken with the man himself, and autographs exchanged.

Before returning to New York, they had their final engagements in Brisbane, where some of the company visited a Koala Bear Zoo, making friends with literally hundreds of the eucalyptus eating mammals. The tour had been a major success and Julie's return to the front line as a soloist had proved more than victorious. She was back at her very best, following the worst and longest lay off she had ever experienced. Yet, another important milestone was waiting to greet her in the early spring of the following year, the kind of surprise package she and the other dancers would never have hoped for in their wildest dreams.

Following a Christmas spent with Joe's parents in Buffalo, New York, the company returned for full ballet classes and rehearsals in preparation for a return to Washington DC. During the previous year, 1980, a Presidential election resulted in Ronald Reagan ousting President Carter from Office. In the spring of 1981, the new President, together with his First Lady, attended at the Kennedy Centre in Washington to watch Dance Ballet Harlem perform, with Julie Felix being one of the soloist dancers. The First Lady, Nancy Reagan, was so impressed by the high standard and quality of the performance she invited the whole company back to the White House for a special dinner given in their honour, to be held on the following night.

After arriving at one of the most famous buildings in the world, situated at 1600, Pennsylvania Avenue, Washington DC, the guests were escorted to the State Dining Room, with all its gold and teak grandeur, rich light brown patterned carpet and floor to ceiling drapes. A large gold chandelier hovered over the white table cloth with cutlery and napkins to match, together with the finest crystal glassware. This was indeed American Capitalism at its very best.

Dress was to be formal and the athletic looking, highly attractive men and women dancers, in their dinner suits and long dresses turned the Presidential seat into one of glamour and excitement.

"Now this is the kind of life I reckon I'm more suited for Julie," Joe whispered, standing proud in his immaculate tuxedo. Julie matched him for his attire with a long flowing, off the shoulder, cream dress with gold trimmings. She wouldn't have looked out of place in that particular room if she'd have been a marble statue on display, looking oh so elegant and oh so beautiful.

They stood, nervously whispering amongst themselves, behind chairs allocated to each member of the company at the long dinner table. The room was filled with anticipation and then hush, when a young man in tails suddenly appeared in front of an open doorway and announced, "Ladies and Gentlemen, the President of the United States and his First Lady."

Julie expected to hear a full orchestra suddenly pipe up with 'The Star Spangled Banner' but instead joined in with the soft applause, as President Reagan stepped through the open doorway, hesitating for a brief second to allow Nancy Reagan to step in front of him. It was all so formal and yet fascinating for every young person present. The atmosphere was relaxed, although there must have been one or two who felt somewhat nervous, wondering whether their Head of State would actually speak with them on a one to one basis.

Of course there was no dancing, but the company members looked like an audience at some magnificent Gala night. It was without doubt the highest point of all of their careers, listening to the country's most powerful man, indeed the most powerful individual in the world; make a short off the cuff speech, welcoming them all into his home, where former Presidents had resided since 1800.

After dinner, the guests were escorted into an anti-room where they finally met and spoke with the President and his First Lady. Both were genuinely appreciative of the artistic skills possessed by these young dancers and Arthur Mitchell in particular was praised for his achievement thus far in offering a helping hand to the impoverished young people of Harlem.

The evening passed by far too quickly, but left each and every one of the invited guests, thrilled and impatient to contact their loved ones afterwards, to share their experiences. On the downside, as the cavalcade drove out of the back entrance of the White House, the obvious poverty and despair amongst the black communities that lived so close to the most photographed mansion in the world brought every member of the company crashing back down to earth.

Throughout 1981 the company spent more time on the road than they did back in New York, the next engagements being in Munich and Spoleto in Italy with every member of DTH living out of their suitcases.

Amazingly, every performance the company gave was always to sell-out crowds and having experienced exactly that same phenomenon in Munich they found the small town of Spoleto just a little different.

The location was situated in the centre of low lying hills, not that far away from Rome, with the majority of the small population living almost on the doorstep of a large impressive cathedral. The Festival dei Due Mondi, meaning the Festival of Two Worlds, was an annual summer music and opera event, having been founded by the composer, Gian Carlo Menotti in 1958. Its purpose was to feature various visual arts, concerts, dance and opera with some drama thrown in, even stretching to roundtable discussions on science. The meaning of the Festival of Two Worlds, given by Menotti, was for the American and European cultures to face each other, and in the June of 1981 the American Dance Theatre Harlem became a part of that spectacle.

The audiences once again fell in love with Arthur Mitchell's dancers, but the real thrill for the company was to follow Mikail Barishnikov with all of their performances in Spoleto. Although Barishnikov was thought by many as a greater ballet dancer than even Nureyev, he was short in stature, which wasn't acceptable by his own country, Russia, which in a way wasn't that far from how Julie had been treated by the British Ballet hierarchy. In Moscow, there was a requirement for the male dancers to tower over the ballerinas and Barishnikov found that to be difficult.

Unlike Nureyev, who defected to the United Kingdom, Basrishikov chose to defect to the USA where he made his fame and money, after being coached by George Ballanchine and to eventually become the Artistic Director of the American Ballet Theatre.

In the same way as Julie had been earlier honoured to dance in a performance which included Rudolf Nureyev, during her final year at Rambert, the complete cast of DTH held similar feelings at being given the opportunity to dance with Basrishikov. And as for her injured foot? What injured foot?

Chapter Twenty-Nine

Dancing in a War Zone

They hadn't quite completely got over wining and dining with the President of the United States, when it seemed that someone with a weird sense of humour had decided to engage the company for a season in Israel, at a time when a war was just about to break out. But there again, The Ballet in its classical dance format, emphasised by grace and the perfection and precision of movement, posture and gestures, should always have its doors open to those who wanted to enter, no matter where they lived, or under what conditions. So, why not Israel, even if it meant performing in flack jackets. As far as Julie was concerned though, it was the most memorable tour she ever undertook.

As the plane was about to touch down in Tel Aviv, the dancers shuddered at the sight of burned out planes, left abandoned on fields that skirted the runway. When the company members finally felt Israeli soil beneath their feet, there were no dignitaries or theatre promoters to greet them, only army personnel comprised of soldiers each carrying automatic sub-machine guns. After being hand searched and frisked for weapons or explosives, the company of ballet dancers from New York were whisked away, under military escort to their sky scraper luxury hotel. Well, at the very least, it was something different to write home about, that was for sure.

As they made that strange journey through the country's capital city, they could sense the unrest and unusual quietness of the Tel Aviv streets. People, who they would normally expect to see hurrying about their daily business were absent, replaced by groups of armed militia and vehicles on deserted street corners. At least the hotel would be a safe haven for them, or so the majority hoped. For the remainder of that travel day, the company rested, noticing the strain etched on the faces of some of the hotel staff. It felt as though they were about to witness history being made in the OK Corral.

The following morning saw the dancers being transported by company bus to the theatre where they were due to perform, an amazing structure, which had been historically named by King Herod in honour of the Roman Emperor, Caesar Augustus. Every five years, the city would host a major sports and Roman games spectacle, which featured Gladiators of that bloody period centuries before. Julie was to be one of those Gladiators, dancing on a stage which dated back to 22 BC, not all that different from the wavy dance floor in the old Church

Hall back in Ealing, where Joyce Butler introduced so many kids to the art of dancing.

The dressing rooms were located underground, in small stone walled caverns that must have been dungeons when the structure was first built, to hold those poor souls waiting to entertain their Roman conquerors with their lives in the open air amphitheatre above. Make shift tables and mirrors had been erected to accommodate the performers and Julie noticed the dancers black boxes had been piled high up against one of the ancient stone walls, in readiness for unpacking. Because of the intense hot atmosphere, rehearsals had to take place early morning and before the sun reached its zenith, from where it could pour its heat waves down on the humans below unmercifully.

The company crew placed the necessary portable ballet barres at strategic points on the stage, as there was no studio and the classes and rehearsals had to be undertaken right there in the open air. When the first class was due to begin, once again, Arthur Mitchell was missing, which created some consternation, the dancers remembering what had taken place on the last occasion the company director had been absent in Mississippi.

As they worked hard and the sun began to rise higher in the sky, Julie felt more like Lawrence of Arabia than a soloist dancer, following the example of others by wrapping a scarf around her head to avoid her scalp from being burnt. After being dismissed each and every one of them was told to stay out of the sun until they were due to return to the theatre at seven o'clock that same evening. Of course, with so much free time handed to them, the holiday mood set in and many of the members made their way to a beach located at the back of the hotel, having been reassured there wasn't much likelihood of an attack being made on that particular side of the city. Others decided to mill around the local shops, while the remainder preferred the air conditioning coolness inside the hotel where they could rest up. Yet Arthur Mitchell still remained absent throughout the remainder of that day, turning what was concern into sheer panic amongst some members of the crew. They became more like a pack of hounds without the sound of a horn to direct them.

When the company bus rolled up to take the performers to the theatre that evening, there was great relief when they caught their first glimpse of Arthur Mitchell, standing at the front of the vehicle, waiting patiently for the dancers to settle in their seats, before addressing them.

"Now you are all aware of what is going on here and that there is a pending war between our hosts and the Palestinians."

Everybody nodded in silence.

"Well, we have to be careful and by that I mean not to forget the situation here is extremely volatile. We can carry on as normal, except I don't want any of you travelling or going anywhere alone, is that understood?"

Again heads nodded in silence, before he sat down and continued the remainder of the journey sitting next to the driver. Good old Mr. Mitchell had managed to add a pinch of drama to the already tense atmosphere, but everybody acknowledged it was right he did so. Any kind of complacency in this place could be dangerous.

The amphitheatre was filling up with their Israeli audience when the company was ushered down to the dungeons, intent on taking advantage of the short space of time they had left, to complete a few stretching exercises. When they eventually entered the open air stage area, the sun was just going down, leaving behind the stifling warmth of the day, which together with the usual heat coming off the stage lights, made it all seem so hot and close. The audience occupied stone semi-circle benches which were curved around the front of the stage, behind which stood a high wall, which was something different altogether.

The dancers couldn't help but feel ill at ease when they first saw, lined up across the top of that high wall, silhouettes of troops grasping machine guns, in readiness to confront any attack coming from the sea. It was macabre and seemingly senseless, although the guests of the ancient Kingdom were well aware that these people were living in fear of losing their country and their lives. Obviously the majority of the Jews living there welcomed military intervention and protection. It was the only Ace they held against would-be invaders and terrorists.

In-between her roles, Julie couldn't help but think about the kind of mixed up world in which she and the others lived in, this was a country at war, but doing its damnedest to continue with life as normal; refusing to allow politics, religion, race or colour or territorial disputes interfere with its social culture or entertainment.

Of course it was difficult for the dancers to give their best, beneath a line of armed soldiers and knowing that any moment a shell might explode near, or right on top of them, or that some missile might just come screaming in with a dozen people's names written on the side, but they did give it their all, and performed for those people, like they had never performed before, each and every one of them. Their courage and dedication was rewarded at the end, when there was an uproar of appreciation and applause from those Israelis gathered around that small stage. Even one or two of the armed guards managed to put their hands together.

After leaving the place of entertainment, the company bus driver made the hotel on two wheels, stopping only for red lights, with his foot pressing down hard on the floor for most of the return journey. Arthur Mitchell warned his dancers not to veer away from the hotel complex and reminded them of that need not to go anywhere alone. Perhaps he thought that Palestinian bombs and missiles were incapable of taking out more than one person at a time.

A stifling hot day had been followed by overheated and dehydrated bodies during the evening's performance, which meant only one thing, once they were all back safely inside the hotel. The bar became a watering hole, so much so, it eventually ran out of soft drinks and jugs of iced water were freely passed around.

During that Israeli tour, Arthur Mitchell became the daddy of them all, his popularity bursting right through the top of the celebrity scale, after he gave the company a day off, having arranged for a tour bus to take them to visit the Holy Land. It was an opportunity not to be missed, although some of the less enthusiastic members preferred to remain resting in the hotel. Nevertheless, Julie in particular couldn't hide her excitement and with Joe hanging on to one arm, was the first on the bus.

How thrilling it was, being driven to actually feast her eyes on all of those sites her mother had told her about when she was a mere child; The place where the Christ child was born; the manger in which Mary and Joseph had sat around bestowing love and adoration upon their son - the Son of God. Her memory delved back to the weekly Sunday School meetings in that same church hall where her life as a dancer had begun, remembering the colour features in various books of Bethlehem, the Three Wise Men and Shepherds and of course, Calvary, where our Lord was finally crucified. And the black girl from Ealing was about to see it all, first hand.

As the tour bus continued through the Israeli countryside, thoughts of war, bombs and missiles were swept aside and the atmosphere amongst the company was one of anticipated joy and excitement. Before starting off early that morning, they had all been warned not to take photographs of the Hasidic Jews and they couldn't help but notice how people looked at them, as they passed by through the many olive groves and settlements, appearing never to have seen black people before, or possibly aliens from another world.

The tourists first stop was to see the Wailing Wall and Julie stood in amazement, staring with inquisitive eyes at the enormous structure with small pieces of paper tucked into various crevices, with men bowing their heads continually and wailing. She felt the need to place a note of her own into the wall, but couldn't find an empty crevice.

Then, all the positive images in her mind vanished, after the dancers and technicians had been escorted through the old walls of Jerusalem. They were all greeted by piles of trash and filth everywhere they looked, it was all so disappointing and sadly disillusionment became the order of a day which had promised so much. The young American black faces stopped at every Station of the Cross, where Christ was supposed to have fallen beneath the heavy cross being carried across his shoulders. Their eyes stared up at every plaque which described every Station, looking at the way in which each plaque had been defaced. Disgusted and ashamed of the mounds of cigarette ends and human urine beneath each plaque. The message was oh so obvious and meaningful to the naïve tourist; ignorance and disrespect was abundant in this part of Israel. In fact, one of the young male dancers wept in despair at what he was witnessing, tasting a flavour of how the believers must have felt on that fateful day, as if history was repeating itself and Christ was actually there once again, falling beneath the weight of his burden.

A visit to the actual place where Jesus was born came next, a small church built over the sight with a small roped off area inside, where the Christ child's manger had allegedly stood. It was all so unreal for Julie who was surprised by the overly ornate interior, with its richness and grandeur atmosphere; unreal considering that Mary and Joseph were paupers. Sadly, the fiction was nothing like the kind of message such an historic location should have been sending out.

More disappointment followed when the company was escorted to Mount Calvary, upon which Christ was crucified, coming away not really believing they had seen the exact location of where the three crosses had once stood beneath a stormy sky. They had been told of so many different places where the incident was supposed to have taken place, a Times crossword puzzle would have been easier to sort out.

But alas, a far lighter moment was to be had when they were then driven through the desert to a site in which the Bedouins lived, an ancient people who apparently hadn't caught up with the modern world, and what a load of tah tah that was. There, far from civilisation, in the middle of nowhere, stood a large tent with a couple of camels parked outside and a television aerial protruding out of the top. At least there was some laughter amongst the group, who were all looking forward to a swim in the Dead Sea.

In fact, they floated rather than swam and actually watched a man reading a newspaper while he just lay there on his back, floating around in a small circle. To think that this part of the world was on the same planet as America was really unthinkable.

Chapter Thirty

The Royal Opera House

Although the majority of the company members had been left disillusioned by their unexpected trip to the Holy Land, all in all they generally felt at least the trip had been a memorable occasion, if only to see a television aerial sticking out of a Bedouin tent. They were all appreciative of Arthur Mitchell's 'man management' and told him so.

The tour had been another success and to celebrate their final night in Israel, some members of the company decided it was only right and fitting to throw a midnight picnic party on the hotel's beach. There was to be no objections to these hard working, globe travelling performers to let their hair down, so, like a bunch of backstreet schoolkids, visiting the seaside for the first time, the air became electric with shouting, screaming and singing. Those of them who fancied a dip or two in the warm sea, did so, performing like a shoal of dolphins. It was all relaxing and enjoyable, a good time being had by all, just like kids playing the wag from school or hiding from the farmer after scrumping apples from his orchard.

Then, those in the sea panicked and ran back towards the beach and those on the beach, dropped everything and flew towards the main hotel building, as a whistling sound flew overhead. Nobody doubted the source of that frightening and threatening shrill, a missile, which was confirmed when it exploded on landing somewhere towards the city centre. The dancers were in shock and the group of serious faces just stared at each other, not really knowing what to say, but certainly anticipating more of those explosive monsters heading their way.

Then Julie's Joe made the moment by just happening to mention that the eastern sky was beginning to turn a shade light than an hour before. That caused more panic than any Palestinian missile could have provoked, because they were all aware they were due to leave the hotel for the airport at 6.0 a.m.

Like a confused herd of running deer, they all grabbed everything in sight and raced inside with sand cluttering up their toes, and clothing and hair dripping wet, only to be met in the foyer by one Arthur Mitchell, standing erect with an expression of scorn on his face, and fear in his eyes.

The company director remained cool and said nothing about the missile attack. Instead, he looked down at his wrist watch and declared, "It is now ten minutes to six o'clock and you all have just ten minutes to board the bus. Anyone not back here by six will be left behind and that is guaranteed."

There wasn't time to dry off, they all threw themselves into lifts to make their respective floors, some thinking the stairs would be quicker, but eventually they all made it within the allotted time and without further admonishment. Goodbye Israel and a sad farewell to a wonderful country torn apart by war. The company were soon holding their hands to their eyes to shield them from the piercing Israeli sun as the plane climbed higher and directly towards it.

After arriving back in the States, it wasn't long before the company was back on the road, listening intently to Three Dog Night, the Bee Gees, Billy Joel and a host of other musical delights as the tour bus made its way across various state boundaries, stopping off at Pasadena, Iowa, Portland, Oregon, Seattle, North Carolina, but to name a few, and still performing in front of packed audiences. But none of those experiences compared with Julie's dream venue, the one theatre she had dreamt of since being a twelve year old child. It came as a complete shock, when Arthur Mitchell gave his dancers the news that they were next appearing back in England at the home of ballet, the Royal Opera House at Covent Garden.

Cheers filled the bus and Julie immediately thought of her mother's dream to one day sing in an opera performed at that very same theatre. But not to worry, Mum, your daughter is about to dance on the very stage you often stared down at in admiration of the artists who played there. On the stage where both Doreen and Julie Felix sat in the cheapest seats in the auditorium, staring down at and gasping at the magnificence of Jessye Norman, all those years ago.

When the company arrived back in London there was something special going on, as if everybody had been belted by a bolt of electricity and had suddenly turned into something super human. During classes and rehearsals, jumps were somehow higher, kicks the same and all round movements accentuated beyond belief. It wasn't just a case of them all trying harder, under Arthur Mitchell and Karl Shook they were already perfectionists, it was the occasion, the theatre, the company notices printed on sheets of paper bearing the royal crest, the critical eye of the audiences they were about to perform before. It all made this particular season special from any other engagement.

She was told to focus on the roles with more intensity as she would be dancing solo, which she did, but there was a surprise awaiting her arrival at the theatre on the first day of class and rehearsals. She had travelled from her parents' house with Joe leaving the tube at the Covent Garden Station. As the couple walked towards the front of the impressive theatre, with its towering white columns and magnificent glass domed roof, Julie suddenly stopped and stared at the main billboard. Were her eyes deceiving her? Was she dreaming all of this and couldn't, didn't want to awaken? There in front of her stood a large poster which contained a picture of herself dancing with one of her partners.

She continued to stare in silence, still unbelieving. This was not a picture of Anna Pavlova, Margot Fonteyn, Evelyn Hart or even Beryl Grey, it was that black girl who couldn't be a part of the line because only white swans were allowed, it was indeed Julie Felix. That specific moment was without doubt the proudest of her life. Everyone would see it; everyone would see that Julie Felix from Ealing, was dancing a lead role in her home town, another blow for those British doubters, who had been so very guilty of burying their heads in the sand. God bless Arthur Mitchell and the backstage prop man who must have fixed the framed picture to the wall.

If the world had been struck by a hundred enormous asteroids and all the land masses became covered by the world's oceans, Julie Felix, daughter of Doreen and Patrick, born in Hammersmith when the snow was falling outside, would have been contented, knowing that she had shown them all that could be achieved, with or without their help.

Her self-indulgence was interrupted by Joe who placed an arm around her shoulders and merely said, "Eh, Julie, that's really something."

She just looked up at him and faintly smiled. Whatever will her parents say?

Still a little shaken with her rubber legs slowly regaining their strength, Julie walked with Joe to the back stage door entrance and both completed the necessary routine of signing in, checking for messages and taking note of their dressing room allocations. Only on this occasion, everything seemed to be so formal with all the notices on the board typed, not scribbled, on sheets of paper bearing the Royal Crest. For a brief moment she wondered whether she had arrived at Buckingham Palace and was to dance in front of the Queen, before Her Majesty endowed her with the title of 'Dame' for her services to the world. Wish on, Julie girl.

Everywhere she stepped and observed, was special to her; the narrow corridors, dance studios and even the changing rooms. The company began its first class in one of the studios, exercising and rehearsing in front of mirrors that stretched from the roof to the basement. The floor had been specially sprung for maximum elevation with a non-slip surface which made dancing a far greater experience, helping to improve Julie's technique even further. She found herself excelling and at ease with the exercises, as she worked her body through the ballet class in similar fashion to moulding clay, warming, elongating and stretching every sinew to the wonderful pieces played on a magnificent grand piano, enjoyed by the company's pianist.

The sound of Arthur Mitchell's voice, "One and two and three and four, higher, more, stronger," inspired his dancers. How Julie loved that man, loved being there and loved her life.

After a fifteen minute break the performers were introduced to the stage for more rehearsals and at last Julie could step out and gaze in adoration of the richness of the large auditorium, dressed in red and gold. In fact there was more gold shining from the balconies than one would find in Aladdin's cave with carpets and curtains to match. She felt as if she had been transported on some magic carpet to a palace, a home for Kings and Queens, but never forgetting who she was and where she'd come from, admiring the glitter and sparkle which she would soon become a part of, dancing with all the grace and agility this Royal place of entertainment demanded. She looked up to the highest seats in the auditorium, where she'd sat as a twelve year old girl, picturing herself and her mother looking down with smiling faces.

It was most certainly the biggest stage she would have ever danced on, which meant she would have to work harder during performances, just to cover the open spaces it offered. What a vivid contrast to the blocks of ancient stone found in the amphitheatre back in Tel Aviv. There wouldn't be any missiles flying overhead either or lines of armed militia looking down on the performers.

It became obvious during rehearsals that Arthur Mitchell was showing slight signs of nervousness and why shouldn't he? The Royal Opera House was similar to Wembley Stadium on Cup Final day when professionals are either made or broken and he was determined his company of dancers would come out of this having won the cup. The work rate was much higher than normal, Mr. Mitchell had something to prove, the company had something to prove, but above all, Julie had the most to prove in front of her home crowd, friends, family and critics on the greatest set in the ballet world.

Various instructions were handed out, including directions that were unusual to say the least, such as dancers having to lift their heads higher than normal because of the extended height of the top balconies where the cheapest seats in the house were made available, Julie and Doreen Felix's seats. Stretching further to cover the whole of the extensive stage floor and so it continued, that first rehearsal never seeming to end, with constant demands being bawled out, "Bigger, higher, head up and project yourselves people. Remember we are in the Opera House now."

Each public performance reached new levels and those who had paid their money to walk past the huge Royal Insignia in the front foyer of the theatre, weren't disappointed by an evening's entertainment provided by the Dance Theatre Harlem. Julie, as usual, gave it everything, feeling strangely at ease and at home in this theatre of theatres, in front of English audiences. She felt as if she was on auto-pilot, mesmerised and transfixed by the overwhelming procession of events that had led her to this apex. They had all trod the same boards before her, Fontaine and Nureyev, Sleep, Pavarotti, to name just a few of the greatest artists the world had seen and that billboard out front had guaranteed everybody was now fully aware of this black girl's genius in a pair of ballet shoes.

One thing was certain, if she had been accepted by Dame Beryl Gray all those years before, if she had joined a British ballet company, remaining in England to dance, she would never have seen or experienced the world stage upon which she had become a fully paid up member, representing her own country of birth in similar fashion to an ambassador.

Of course she managed to spend some time with Mom and Dad and they confirmed yet again, how proud they were of their youngest daughter, but as soon as the season ended in Covent Garden, it was time to get back to New York to unpack, do some washing and refill the suitcase. The next port of call was to be Tokyo and yet another jet setting experience waiting around the corner, a far cry from the Royal Opera House, London, England.

Chapter Thirty-One

Parisian Racism

Japan appeared to be a country which ran like clockwork, with a population whose vocabulary didn't include the word 'late', so everybody had to be punctual where ever they travelled during that tour, as a mark of respect to those who treated them all as if they were royalty. The public enthusiasm that followed Dance Theatre Harlem was close to fanaticism, causing the dancers to enjoy the rock star adoration, in similar fashion to how they had been received in Hong Kong.

They were greeted at the stage door, following each performance by mobs of screaming fans, jostling and demanding autographs, reaching out in the hope they would touch one of these performers who had come from so far away in the western world. A coach had to be booked to transport the company to and from the hotel as any thought of Shanksie's Pony was out of the question, security being a priority.

On opening night in Tokyo, fans actually chased after the bus, screaming nice things in Japanese, or so the dancers thought, asking for autographs by waving various signature books at the windows of the coach. Of course, professional dancers perform with the intention of pleasing those watching and such mass appreciation began to swell a few heads, making all that DTH did, well worthwhile.

"Okay, fellers, I was thinking of hiring me a couple of heavies, just to watch over me while I went out to get a glass of Sack Me."

"You mean Sake don't you, bud?"

"Nope, because if Mr. Mitchell gets to know what's in my head with all those Japanese girls chasing us, he'll want to sack me."

After the Tokyo engagements, the company was booked to travel on the Bullet Train to Kyoto, which whipped them across Japan at 125 miles an hour, with Julie thinking that her life had travelled at just about the same speed. There was no time to draw breath, with forty plus stomachs being usually left behind where they'd boarded the train. As soon as the performance had gone down in Kyoto, they were off again, on that flying Bullet Train to Kobe, which to the exhausted dancers might just as well have been on the moon. Eyes were heavy, bodies retreating and feet screaming for respite. Even the Station Masters at each stop, dressed in immaculate uniforms with white gloves, failed to lift the spirits. New York and feather beds were so far away at that particular moment.

Following the Japanese tour, they finally returned to their home town of the Big Apple, appreciating Arthur Mitchell's decision to give each and every one of them a couple of days rest. But when the company returned to work, the kind of news that awaited them, left them all aghast. Mitchell informed his people that they were to fly out again, but this time to Denmark where a film production company would be waiting for them. Dance Theatre Harlem was going to consist of film stars, having been chosen to play a major dancing role in a dance film based on the Brando movie, A Streetcar Named Desire. That did the trick, and if there had been any of the cast thinking about asking for more time off, then they would have been certified as being half a sandwich short of a picnic.

Julie was asked to play the lead role of 'Stella' which required certain acting skills which suited the English speaking girl who just loved to act. In fact, if Julie hadn't been drawn into professional dancing as a career, she would have no doubt, been flying her kite in the dramatic world of impersonation. It was a challenge requiring the need for depth of passion, which was no stranger to her, as passion had always been at the forefront of her dancing, but acting on screen was far different from acting live on stage and that was the real challenge. She would be performing to a camera, a black hole without personality or any kind of facial expression.

The filming took place in a small studio with a movie director over lording it above Arthur Mitchell, who was made to sit back and watch his company receive instructions that were more in tune with having to perform in a smaller space, in front of a variety of background scenery.

The dancers wardrobe consisted more of street clothing to fit in with the film, but following a number of 'takes' the parts the company played was deemed a success. They were allowed to see the finished film in a private studio and after release the dance version of A Streetcar Named Desire was nominated for an Emmy Award.

When the company arrived in Paris to continue another tour following their break to complete the filming in Denmark, they found things were altogether much different and were returned to earth with a thud. The Parisians, thought to have been extremely knowledgeable and enthusiastic about any kind of entertainment with a classical label stuck on it, proved to be totally ignorant of what DTH was about, wallowing in widespread racism.

In fact the negative French response to an all-black dancing company from New York was not just unexpected, but demoralising, leaving the company distraught and having a great deal of difficulty to motivate themselves. The dancers performed in front of poor attendances which showed little appreciation of the artistry demonstrated, which was amazingly difficult to understand as DTH had never before danced anywhere that wasn't a packed out theatre. But, the French were the French and it was their prerogative to boycott any entertainment, classical or otherwise, if that's what they were about.

Where-ever Julie went in Paris, she was met with derision, prejudice and condescension. Whether waiting to be served at a cosmetics counter in one of the large stores or sitting in a restaurant on the Champs-Elysees, she always had to wait until every other customer had been served and would only attract the attention of the waiter or shop assistant by asking for some attention in French. And even then she would be told to speak in English. Condescending? Absolutely. Racist? They were certainly a people who wouldn't have been out of place, or gone-amiss living in Mississippi.

So, the company left the French city of culture, having been made to feel they had contracted some kind of disease, which the Parisians were frightened to death of catching. Thank God for the humble and warm feeling, gained from just stepping into a yellow cab back in New York, their own city of culture.

Shortly after returning to their home town, the company was back on the road, heading for a return visit to Pasadena, which always brought back memories of their encounter with Michael Jackson. Only this time, they were told their performance was to be watched by yet another super star, Prince. Okay, so perhaps it wasn't quite the same kind of thrill they got from meeting up with the pop icon himself, the humble and polite master of both song and dance, but they still anticipated there would be some excitement in meeting Prince. Only they didn't meet him. In fact they never saw his face.

"My boy has to stay incognito see," his road manager announced during the stage rehearsal "It's the publicity you see; in truth he's just a shy kind of guy."

Well, just before curtain Prince arrived at the theatre incognito, with a bright purple sequin covered dazzling gown hanging over his head that had also some gold trimming thrown in. The apparition looked more like a pro wrestler doing his best to gee up the paying punters. The only thing from which that particular super star would have been incognito was a colour blind artist who painted in oils.

In 1983 Julie and Joe were given time off to visit Julie's home in Ealing, London to finally tie the knot. Joe's father had initially been cautious about his son being married to a black girl, in fact, at one stage he totally rejected the idea, but after time and a few meetings with Julie, he was quietly won over and actually began to like the girl, after discovering that black people didn't actually live on bananas and could indeed speak English the same as anyone else. But it was yet another rejection Julie had to manage and try hard not to affect her own non-bias attitude and thoughts.

Two people in love were married in a small church in Ealing and both family and friends celebrated vociferously, as the newlyweds left the church as man and wife, including two friends Julie and Joe had invited from DTH. The couple spent their one week's honeymoon in Devon, keeping well away from shark fishing boats, well any kind of boats if it came to that. But sadly, as is usually the case when two lovers are so engrossed with one another, the rain poured down and then some, throughout the whole time they were there. Sitting on a wall, looking out across the waves heading towards them and the grey unfriendly sky and eating fish and chips from newspaper, with drops of rain trickling down their necks, it was all a far cry from Oregon, New Hampshire, Iowa and every other sun blessed city they had previously performed in.

But they were in love and far from the madding crowd, the different colour of their skins being way off the agenda as far as they were concerned. There could be no repercussions about racial prejudice or rejections thrown Julie's way, as she had ploughed her way through those particular mine fields. They had each other and that was all that mattered.

Chapter Thirty-Two

The Streets of New York

When the newlyweds returned to New York, Julie felt somehow different, apathetic and very melodramatic. Such feelings had nothing to do with her dancing or her career, she realised she was once again missing home. She was now a married woman, wed to an American man and her permanent home was to be in the Big Apple. That apathy seemed to stay with her during the first few weeks back at work in Harlem. She once again began to yearn for a green and pleasant landscape that wasn't Central Park. Of course she talked to Joe about how she felt, but what could either of them do? The only sound advice she was given was that time was a great healer and eventually her down side would come to terms with her new, permanent American life style.

She was tied to one of the most popular ballet companies in the world, in fact she'd travelled the world, she'd witnessed with her own eyes, a devastating volcanic eruption, stood staring out at Caribbean sunsets, seen Manhattan grind to a standstill in a power cut and freak snowstorm. On top of all that, the girl from Ealing had also watched a young black man be blown away on the streets of Harlem, met the most powerful man on earth and his First Lady, adding rock stars and other famous people to her list of personal achievements. So, why did she still feel the kind of heart ache reserved for children and young people leaving home for the first time? There wasn't any immediate answer, except yes, time was probably the only friend she had to help with her dilemma. If only her parents lived just around the corner, bringing with them a small piece of what she knew as England.

Shortly after starting back at DTH it was one early summer's evening when Julie and another girl from the dancing school, were walking down Columbus Avenue, both engrossed in an intellectual conversation discussing whether American chocolate bars were as good and those you could purchase in England. The girls noticed a black limousine cruising along the curb-side, just behind them. They became unnerved, wondering what the hell the driver was up to, so they dived into a nearby newsagent's shop and waited in anticipation of perhaps a robbery about to go down.

Then a man wearing wire rimmed spectacles stepped inside the same shop, and began eyeing the two girls, apparently buying nothing from the vendor. Julie gripped her friend's arm tight and whispered in her ear, "We might get caught up here in a shooting or armed robbery," continuing to look busy studying the chocolate section. Thank God the man then left the shop and both girls relaxed.

After buying some confectionery, and satisfied the brief crisis had ended, they turned to leave just as another man entered the shop, dressed smartly in a black suit, wearing a large pair of shades. He stopped the two girls and quietly said, "Excuse me girls." That was all, before he handed to Julie an impressive looking business card, turned and walked out of the shop.

The girls read the card and on one side was printed 'R. DeNiro', on the reverse side was a small handwritten message, 'Would you ladies do me the honour of having dinner with me."

After staring at the card for a few seconds, they both screamed out aloud before Julie turned to her friend and said in an excited voice, "What the hell would my Joe think of this? I'm a married woman now." It was obvious the man in the suit had been the super star, Robert DeNiro.

They eventually left the shop on shaky legs and the black limo had disappeared. Such an incident could only have happened in New York, well perhaps California as well, but there was yet another famous name to add to Julie's list, which would come later.

The non-stop blaring of sirens going on virtually twenty four hours a day, plus those screaming yellow cabs with drivers constantly stopping and shouting, "What the hell are you pal, tired of living or summat?" This became more frequent every time an attempt was made to cross Fifth Avenue, which finally made Julie decide to move out of the city, somewhere much quieter. Working, playing and living in New York had suddenly lost its magic and she discussed the idea with her new husband.

The couple moved out of Manhattan to New Jersey, intending to commute to the city. Dance Theatre Harlem was uptown in Harlem and the George Washington Bridge linked New Jersey with their place of work, so they lashed out as much as they could in dollars and embarked on the property ladder. The apartment they purchased left them with some money to spare, which they used to purchase a brand new Toyota Celica saloon motor car. It was all so adventurous and both Julie and Joe felt that they were achieving and going places, at long last.

Shortly after vacating the city, Joe began to teach his young wife how to drive the Toyota, which wasn't the greatest idea he'd ever had, with Julie trying hard to ignore the thrills and frights associated with a novice driver moving about on Manhattan highways. On occasions she felt like a mouse trapped between two tom cats arguing about which was going to have first swipe at the supper that shivered before them. Joe yelling various instructions and cabbies doing their best to unnerve the female driver with their screams and yells, not to mention the finger salutes she received by the minute.

It all came to a head when Joe was back behind the wheel, driving from New Jersey towards the city, when they suddenly found themselves at the tail end of a not so uncommon queue of traffic. They were both sat staring out of the window, looking at nothing in particular, when a large van suddenly crashed into their rear boot. Julie was instantly angry, but said nothing. Joe was crying, having just seen the back of their brand new car turned into a scrap metal dealer's dream. So, to help temper his anger, he shook a fist at the driver of the offending van, who in response climbed out of his vehicle and moved towards the Toyota, shouting and screaming abuse, with a baseball bat in one hand.

"Don't get involved, Joe," begged Julie, already winding the windows up and locking the doors.

"I'll kill the bastard," said Joe, who was about half the size of this Goliath who was getting too close for comfort.

"Please, Joe."

The van driver began to hammer at the doors and windows before staring at Julie and screaming as loud as his foul mouth could echo the words out, "Who the fuck are you, hanging around with some black woman?" So much for non-racist behaviour and equality for all those living in the Big Apple.

Then, as Goliath was really beginning to shake up his emotions and scrambled illiterate brain, Julie noticed the traffic in front of them had cleared and shouted to Joe to drive. He did so, putting his foot down on the floorboards, causing the obese apparition to fall over backwards, planting his rump in a fairly deep puddle.

They stopped at the first police station they came across and both went inside to report the incident. An old desk sergeant with silvery hair shook his head and rolled his eyes, before sharing with the young couple some fatherly advice, obviously based on his vast experience of having been a street cop.

"Now, feller," he drawled, "This is what you've got to do. Go and get yerself the biggest baseball bat money can buy and next time you get dressed down in your car, hit the bastard over the head with it before he gets you, got the message." So much for law abiding citizens and basic common sense.

Joe and Julie soon settled in New Jersey, living the life of a normal married couple at night and then having to work hard to transform themselves back into athletic figures during the day at DTH. Then, during the summer of 1984 the couple were both on the road again, this time they were to perform at the London Coliseum. Tours to England were always an obvious joy for Julie, because seeing her parents again was such a bonus.

As the plane left the runway from Kennedy Airport, the company members were chatting away as usual, Julie and Joe telling those nearest to them about a funny episode that they had witnessed outside a favourite Korean grocery store of theirs near where they lived. While the couple had been selecting from a magnificent display of fruits and vegetables from outside the front of the shop, to later prepare for their evening meal, there was a sudden scream that came from inside. It hadn't been a woman's scream but a man's, and suddenly the male owner of the shop came running out onto the street and with a terrified look on his face, shouted at the two dancers, "God Almighty, the missus, she mad in the head, she say I go with other woman."

Just then a large woman with biceps similar to a navvy's and an apron tied around her bulging waist also came out of the shop, towering over the small, thinly built Korean, who cowered, holding an arm up defensively. But, it obviously wasn't his day and his Gods had deserted him. The woman hit him over the head with a twelve egg frying pan, so large, even Joe couldn't have picked it up. The sound echoed to across the street, causing other shoppers to stop and watch.

"Get inside you fornicating son of a ragman's daughter," she bellowed, and the little man, now crying his eyes out, shuffled to seek shelter back behind his own counter.

"As she got something against ragmen?" Joe asked humorously.

"I'm not sure," Julie replied, "But I'll be damned if she hasn't got something against her old man."

Everybody who overheard the tale laughed as the plane gathered height and it was then that Julie and a few others realised something was wrong. One of the engines seemed to intermittently cough and groan and then it felt that they'd hit some turbulence, a lot of turbulence.

"Welcome on board our flight today," a voice rang out over the intercoms, "We are having a small problem at the moment with one of our engines, but there's no need for alarm, we are working on solving this small problem, but for safety reasons will be returning to JFK as soon as we have a little more height."

Sod that!

Well, most of the passengers didn't know whether to smile, cry, or scream out in terror. A 'small problem' to the pilot of this crate might be what he honestly believed, but to the uninitiated, which meant just about every other person on board, in particular the DTH company, this lot had disaster written all over it.

Stewardesses were all over them like mustard on a hamburger,

"Please remain in your seats and keep your seat belts fastened, there's no need for alarm."

"I have to make the John, miss."

"Sorry, sir, but the captain doesn't think it will be long before we're back on the ground, can you possibly wait?"

"No, I really need to make the John, miss."

"Won't be long now, sir."

"Well then, miss, you'd better go and fetch a mop."

At that the small cherub like man stood up and pissed all over the centre aisle, an obvious look of embarrassment across his ruddy complexion.

"My God, the filthy animal," one woman shouted out.

"Well the feller did ask for the John," another man answered back.

Then the plane hit the runway with a thump and the flight had returned back to Kennedy Airport.

"That was quick," one man said, "And thanks for the entertainment, feller," he said to the small piss artist who had quickly tried to make himself invisible by struggling down the aisle to the rear exit door.

They could all hear the wailing sirens and see the red flashing lights encircling their plane as it came to a final standstill and for safety reasons had to slide down inflated chutes to get down to the ground. Unfortunately, the plane had lost an engine but the fault had made itself known when the pilot still had the option to return to base. Perhaps another few minutes into the flight, when the plane was dividing the skies at thirty six thousand feet, things might have been different. Anyway, they were all soon back in the VIP lounge safely, which was all that mattered.

Another replacement flight was soon on the tarmac and although the dancers and technicians from Dance Theatre Harlem were very concerned about having to go skywards again, they were all soon crossing the Atlantic Ocean without further incident. At least there would be yet another exciting tale to tell the grand kids.

Chapter Thirty-Three

Olympic Games 1984

The first sighting of her parents told Julie how much they had both aged during the past twelve months, as if life's most troubling difficulties had finally taken their toll. Her father's hair had turned grey, he looked drawn and tired and her mother appeared smaller in height, highlighted by a stoop in her back, as if she'd been carrying heavy bags of coal throughout the time Julie had been absent. For the first time in her life, she realised just how elderly her parents were getting and although she felt some sadness, she loved them both even more dearly. They were without doubt, the real gem stones in her life and always had been.

The most prominent change she saw, however, was in Patrick and the pride in her father's eyes when he held his daughter close. That was the knockout punch that floored Julie. The promise she had made to herself many years before, to repay her father for all he had given her, had been fulfilled, she would have swapped all those visits and performances in those countries covering the globe for just that one moment.

During the next few days, there was little time to spend at her parents' home, the work schedule being frantic. Dance Theatre Harlem were about to premier their version of the classical ballet, Giselle, which had been set in the American deep State of Louisiana, rather than the original Austrian version staged by a fellow Brit, Frederic Franklin. The show was an overwhelming success and DTH became the first American company to win the Lawrence Olivier Award for best dance production of the year. Congratulations and well done everybody.

After a very short visit to London, the company was soon on its way back to home base in New York and throughout that return trip, Julie couldn't help but be concerned about her parents' health, having seen them age so unbelievably quickly over a such a short period of twelve months. In fact, shortly after returning to her New Jersey home, she received news from her mother that Patrick was indeed suffering from stomach cancer.

She so badly wanted to catch the next flight home, but couldn't, unless she wanted to prematurely bring an end to her career. She felt useless, being over three thousand miles away from her parents who had no support or help. It was no wonder her mother looked so done in and tired with life. Her sister, Lucia, was also missing from home, still living in Greece and tied to her restaurant there, although Julie had maintained contact with her and was well aware of many of the problems her sister was having to deal with herself.

Eventually, the proud man from Saint Lucia in the West Indies, the same man who had named his first born after the island of his birth, was taken ill, resulting in half of his cancerous stomach being removed. What the surgeons never told him was that they' had taken half of his soul away at the same time, and Patrick was never the same man again, although at least the operation had bought him some more time to admire his brightly painted front door and boast of his girl Julie to the neighbours.

The main reason Julie couldn't return home was that DTH had been booked for one of their most prestigious performances in their history, which was to dance as a support group to Lionel Ritchie at the closing ceremony of that year's 1984 American Olympic Games, dancing to his song, 'All Night Long'. They had also been booked to perform at the same ceremony, George Balanchine's ballet, 'Stars and Stripes'.

The thrill and excitement of such an engagement, dancing in front of millions of people all the world round, swept through the company and everybody practiced and rehearsed with the kind of vigour and concentration reserved for such high profile performances. Julie was an exception and couldn't hide the worry and concern about her father, finding it difficult to concentrate and display her normal, happy, motivating and enthusiastic usual self. But of course she gave it everything she had, not faltering and maintaining her usual highest level of professionalism throughout the preparation.

Finally the scene was set, the athletes had tasted victory and failure, the medals had been won and lost, the accusations made and withdrawn and now it was the time when the whole of Los Angeles would play host to the rest of the world in one of the most memorable closing ceremonies in Olympic history, to be held at the Olympiad Arena.

Stars and Stripes were everywhere, red, blue and white, lighting up the sparkling darkness of the night air and embracing the merriment and pride which filled the arena. The music blasted out as the star singer, Lionel Ritchie, danced his way to the centre of the packed out stadium and sang that wonderful ballad, 'All Night Long', hesitating half way through, as the red and white glittering costumes of the DTH dancers suddenly appeared and displayed their dazzling dance talents to all that watched. The majestic performance lasted almost ten minutes, making history for a solo singer at a closing ceremony of the games.

For the Dance Theatre Harlem, for every person involved in putting on such glamour and talent, the night was a major success, a hard act to follow as they say. At the end, Julie and the rest of the dancers were proud and stood tall when the plaudits were handed out, but although she had danced with conviction and strength, she had danced with a hollow feeling in her stomach. Following that closing ceremony, each of those who took part in the Ritchie history making performance were awarded with a bronze Olympic Medal.

After the Olympics came disaster for Julie. The company returned to San Francisco, where the usual daily rationing of earthquakes still seemed to be taking place, a rumble here and a rumble there and a rumble inside Julie's stomach. She fell sick with her joints stiffening up and she was haemorrhaging heavily.

She was rushed into hospital where she was told she was pregnant but having a miscarriage. The effect on Julie was devastating, although she and Joe hadn't been planning at starting a family at that stage of their lives, because of their individual careers, it had happened and the result of the loss of a child was catastrophic as far as Julie was concerned. She became unsettled and depressed, knowing that a baby, a human being had been growing inside her and she had lost it. She was put on anti-depressants and told to rest up. The inevitable happened of course, when the company went on tour without her. Memories were triggered of the hard time she had dealt with after so badly injuring her foot in that career threatening accident.

She stood by, feeling a mixture of emotions as DTH were awarded with all kinds of different honours, including their first season at the Metropolitan Opera House to celebrate the company's tenth year with the First Lady and Mayor of New York. It was certainly hard for Julie to watch from a distance and bite into her bottom lip. But she was a fighter, as she had proved before, and by God she would return, return with a vengeance, as she done had before. As always, she followed the medical advice to the letter and stayed away from the studio, but having completed her enforced remedial isolation, returned, refreshed with all rockets firing. Sweat, toil, pain and commitment once again returned and her full recovery was soon achieved, although in her mind, she felt perhaps one more performance would probably bring her nearer to the closing chapter of her illustrious career.

PART FIVE

The Final Curtain

Chapter Thirty-Four

The Performance of Her Life

The great tenor's voice reached out to all four corners of the theatre and to the highest balcony, with the audience in total silence, mesmerised by the deep and rich sounds produced by the master.

"...I've the soul of a millionaire. From time to time two thieves steal all the jewels out of my safe, two pretty eyes.

They came in with you just now, and my customary dreams my lovely dreams, melted at once into thin air.

But the theft doesn't anger me, for their place has been taken by hope.

Now that you know all about me, you tell me who you are.

Please do..." Che gelida manina from Puccini's La Boheme.

As the magic of Luciano Pavarotti touched everyone present in the Metropolitan Opera House, New York, a figure suddenly appeared behind the greatest tenor of them all, a graceful ballerina who spread her wings and flittered across the stage, dressed in olive green to blend in with the background forest scenery. The performance of the elf like dancer attracted four thousand pairs of staring eyes like a magnet, four thousand pairs of ears tuning into the master's beautiful and rich singing voice and those eyes watching the magical and breath taking ballerina, moving with the refinement and elegance of a shadow with wings. Two performances blending into one that reached the very height of Opera and Classical Ballet, creating one unbelievable and unforgettable presentation.

At the end, those who had been so fortunate to have seen such a wonderful spectacle stood on their feet like excited children, so thrilled, so captivated by what they had just witnessed, only screams could be verbally delivered, turning to cheers and uproar which changed the auditorium into a cell filled with human gratitude and amazement. The conductor rose to acknowledge the applause, but all eyes were on Pavarotti. The wonderful, outstanding ballerina, that fairy from another world who had embellished the performance, had vanished as quickly as she had appeared, like a ghost returning to the invisible curtain of mist and fog that was filled with artistic finesse which paid tribute to this particular famous stage.

Not one person present in that great and majestic place of entertainment that night, had any idea the girl who had given them so much enchantment, so much amazement, had stepped from the shadows of the corps de ballet, having returned from a prolonged serious illness to fulfill her dream as a soloist ballerina. To dance with the greatest operatic singer ever to walk this earth.

Alas, Julie's time had finally come. All the years of toil and success had ganged up to give her a message, one that confirmed the ticking clock was ringing for time out. London's Big Ben boomed out on the quarter of each hour, public houses rang a bell at closing time, The famous cricket ground at Lords rang a bell at the beginning of each day of a test match, but for Julie, the ringing tone wasn't marking the beginning, only the ending, only the time when that ticking time bomb inside every man and woman, suddenly went off, telling them that finally their time had come to stop. She was emotionally drained; her body was beginning to turn its back on further physical punishment, telling her it could not possibly behave in a similar way to her last performance, ever again. Her limbs had given their all and like a motor car without fuel, could no longer continue.

She still looked as young, slim and graceful as she had appeared during her three years at Rambert, but her heart was older, much older. Her desire was to continue, but even her deepest wish was now being confronted by an impossible mine field. She tried to shake it off, she tried to continue with sincerity and determination, like a race horse that had broken its leg and worked in earnest to get back up, but couldn't.

Julie talked it through with Joe, until the early hours of the morning and he was understanding, but with all the options and ideas and suggestions in the world, they both knew that Julie's age had caught up with her and there was nothing in this world that could be done. There are a million creams and ointments available to hide the ageing process, skilled surgeons who can remove lines and disfigurement, but there is no one or no thing on the planet that can restore a body back to its youth and make it capable of continuing at the same level as the professional ballet dancer.

Soccer players with fast legs move to the midfield as a certain age approaches, before finally having to succumb to the physical demands put on them. So do professional dancers, no matter how talented they have become, except there is no midfield for them and no place to hide. So, it came to the point where Julie had to make the decision and did so. She would retire from the stage and she and her husband would return to England to raise a family, an English family, but first she would speak to Arthur Mitchell.

She stood in the very same office in which Mr. Mitchell had handed over a brand new, exciting and thrilling life to the black girl from Ealing Her voice was quiet and dispirited as she told him of her decision to quit, to resign, give in her notice, it all meant the same thing, she was leaving DTH.

"Have you properly thought this through, Julie?" this amazing man quietly asked her, with the kind of sadness and surprise in his eyes that told her she had been one of his few chosen children, one of his beloved dancers in which there had been a bond, the only kind that could have existed in such a hard and demanding profession as they had both enjoyed together.

There were tears in her eyes when she answered, "Yes, I wish I didn't have to leave, but I just cannot go on."

Then Arthur Mitchell surprised her by offering her a contract as a Ballet Mistress with his company, which confirmed the kind of respect and admiration he held for this girl of his, this girl who was about to leave the nest. But, deep down, Julie knew she had to go, she had to return home to England, no matter how much pain and grief she felt. She turned him down, just as she had done so all those years ago, back in London when he'd made the first approach and the company had an engagement at the Royal Variety Performance. That was ten years earlier which to Julie seemed more like a hundred years before.

He stepped from behind his desk and held her, embracing her with utter sadness and sincerity. She held on to him in the same way she had took Angela Ellis into her arms on her last day at Rambert.

"Well, if you've made your mind up, the very best of luck to you," were his final words before kissing her on one cheek and returning to his desk to carry on with his work, in the only way Arthur Mitchell could.

Julie slowly turned and walked out of the office, never to return. Her life as a professional ballerina was at an end and as she collected her equipment from the changing rooms, a million memories of a long and fascinating, magical journey began to fill her mind. The ghosts of the past flittered across her memories like whispers. That creased friendly face of Sam the cabbie; the young, 'Where you going, sister', black kid, mown down on the streets of Harlem; the gloved hand of Michael Jackson as he reached to touch her and the applause, a thousand hands clapping together in unison. All briefly appearing behind a transparent curtain of clouded mesh.

There were no more tears as she stepped out of the studio on to the Harlem streets, still holding her head up high, remembering that first day she had walked the same route, shuffling her feet along the side walk, nervously staring across at the netball park and praying she wouldn't be taken advantage of. It was all so very sad, but as she had done so many times before, her decision for her future was now set in concrete and there would be no going back.

Mr. and Mrs. Cipolla caught their plane to Heathrow without looking back, although it was difficult not to feel some despondency. Of course, Joe's life also had to change, leaving DTH and moving with his wife back to London, where they lived with Julie's parents for a short while before getting an apartment near Richmond. But, Joe's days in the ballet weren't numbered and he continually looked for a position in England. After all, he had a wife to support.

Luck came their way when he managed to fill a gap at Sadler's Wells Royal Ballet, who had been looking for a soloist male dancer, but at the age of thirty, Julie's career was well and truly over. The good news for them both was when Julie returned home for the final time, she was three months pregnant and when she told Doreen and Patrick they were to be grandparents, the small house in Ealing filled with joy and excitement. The kind of welcoming feelings that were long overdue.

Chapter Thirty-Five

Friends and Loved ones

The ten years Julie Felix spent with the Dance Theatre Harlem, the experiences she gained as a worldwide jet setter, representing her country where ever she performed, would be difficult for anyone to forget and is still a part of her today. If fate had decided she would be accepted in her own country and become a professional dancer for a British company, there is little doubt she would have enjoyed the same eye opening wonders she actually saw first-hand. There is little doubt she would have been capable of displaying her talent, her British made talent, on such a wide theatrical stage.

Before she left America, her fellow dancers threw a party for the English ballerina and she surprisingly pined for the American way of life for a long time after leaving, a life in which she had shared so many incredible times. But the question always remained with her, why when America held her in such esteem, did not her own country? Julie Felix never received an award or recognition for what she achieved by carrying the Union Jack as far away as Hong Kong and Japan, giving so much pleasure to so many people of different nationalities. She embraced the fears and anxieties of a people living in a war torn country, through her magical artistic talent, people who were at that time, constantly battling to prevent hostilities from breaking out.

Just one year after returning to England, she was employed by the Sadler's Wells Theatre as a ballet teacher and both she and Joe moved into an apartment that went with their positions and was located in the theatre itself. In 1988 she became the company teacher and remedial coach for the same theatre and her husband Joe performed as a principle dancer under Sir Peter Wright the director.

In 1986, Julie Felix was awarded a place in the 44th edition of the Marquis publication of 'Who's Who in America'.

In 1989, Julie visited her sister at her beach restaurant on Zakynthos in the Greek Islands and was initially impressed by the way Lucia ran her business. She was also surprised that her sister had developed a talent for creating culinary delights, but Julie also noticed for the first time how Lucia had begun to drink heavily, a large glass of the local wine not being too far away, even when she was working. After all, this was a Greek Island in the sun; where work, fun and happiness joined forces, but what the former ballerina didn't realise at that time was her sister had already started on a downward path which would eventually result in alcoholism.

Shortly after Julie's visit, Lucia surprisingly turned her back on Zakynthos and returned home to live for a while with her parents. Although the drinking continued, Patrick and Doreen remained proud of their eldest daughter and in fact, Patrick decided to take Lucia with him on one of his two yearly visits back to the place of his birth, Saint Lucia in the West Indies.

Both father and daughter spent two weeks on holiday at Patrick's place of birth, but some unexplained serious disparity took place between them and they returned home, in verbal isolation from each other. Sadly the rift between father and daughter went deep and following their return to Ealing, a black cloud hung over the family home for a long time to come.

No one knew the reason for the falling out; no one ever became aware of whatever happened during that short period of time in Saint Lucia, but Patrick disowned his daughter and the reason for that was taken by both to their graves. Not long after returning from Saint Lucia, Julie's sister returned to the West Indies where she worked in a restaurant owned by Lord Glenconner, more popularly known as Colin Tennant, friend and confidante of the Queen's sister, Princess Margaret. The restaurant was named 'Bang between the Pitons,' after two volcanic mountains which stand like tall centurions, overlooking Jalousie Bay which is situated on the south western coast of Saint Lucia.

She gained more catering experience at the highest level and coupled with that, and of course her business knowledge sourced from the beach restaurant in Zakynthos, a point was reached where she felt she was ready to once again, go it alone.

She eventually opened another small restaurant on Saint Lucia and at first, worked hard, bringing to the tables more unique dishes created from her own innovation and now vast experience of cooking. Lucia's reputation was spreading, her new business venture bringing more financial success, as was the increasing volume of alcohol she flirted with on a daily basis.

Slowly her craving for drink began to take over the need to continue running her new found business as a priority, and once again, life for the girl from Ealing began to take a downward spiral. The restaurant soon hit upon difficulties, such as unpaid bills and fewer clients and she was finding it harder to find the necessary commitment and ability to work. There was no help or support for her and eventually the inevitable happened and Lucia was forced to close the restaurant and head back to the United Kingdom, penniless and plagued by alcoholism.

The Sadler's Wells Ballet was granted a Royal Charter and later became the Sadler's Wells Royal Ballet, before being taken over by Birmingham Council and having its name changed to the Birmingham Royal Ballet in 1990. Julie agreed to move with the company up to

Birmingham, remaining as the company teacher and remedial coach. When she told her parents of the move her father was pessimistic, explaining, "Julie, I've never been further north than Watford Gap and I'm not moving up to Scotland now, that's a fact girl."

The new Birmingham Royal Ballet was launched with a Gala opening night at the newly built Birmingham Hippodrome with Princess Diane attending to watch Hobson's Choice, a ballet choreographed by David Bintley. The stage production was later turned into a film which again was watched by the Princess at a private screening.

Just after that event, Julie was invited to present some awards to young dancers attending Joyce Butler's School of Dance in Ealing. She enjoyed the trip back to where her roots were and following the presentations, visited her parents, where she found her father confined to his bed in a serious and worrying condition. Without hesitation, Julie made him get dress and drove him straight to hospital.

At first, mother and daughter were told that Patrick had a chest infection, but not being happy with that, Julie demanded a chest Xray and the result was devastating. Patrick had cancer in both lungs, which appeared to be advanced. He was given some medical attention and told he could return home until a specialist became available.

When they returned home, as he climbed out of the car, Patrick being Patrick, offered his daughter £20 to pay for petrol and for taking him to hospital and transporting him back home.

Julie felt distraught at her father's offer and told him, "Dad, I would do anything for you, I love you."

Patrick just nodded and stepped towards the creaky gate at the front of his house, before suddenly turning and speaking in a feeble voice, "You know, Julie, I love you as well and I'm very proud of you." He then turned and walked towards that brightly coloured door he was so proud of.

Julie was in tears and held her face in both hands. This took place on a Sunday, on the following Wednesday, Julie's mother rang to tell her that Patrick had died. The sight of her father, walking through that old squeaky gate was the last she saw of him, but more importantly, those few words he'd uttered to his daughter, who throughout her life had desperately wanted, needed her father's love and pride, were the last words he ever spoke to her.

By the time Lucia returned home from the island of her father's birth, Patrick had sadly died without there ever being any opportunity for them to repair whatever differences had driven them away from each other in the past. Lucia was diagnosed with liver disease and went to live with her mother, who by then had moved to the Midlands town of Wootton Wawen to be closer to Julie.

As Lucia's health continued to deteriorate, those around her felt helpless, including Julie who prayed and yearned for her sister to rid herself of the tyrant that was slowly destroying her life. The drinking continued, the nightmares becoming more frequent and the weight loss devastatingly abhorrent. The release the so talented Lucia was seeking from her enslaver, was far away, hidden beneath a thick blanket of fog, which strengthened more and more as each day passed.

Lucia's physical deterioration got worse and Julie sobbed in defeat of her efforts to help her sister. Words of advice, suggestions of support and intolerance of the disastrous route upon which Lucia was hell bent on following, never dried up. But both Julie and her mother, Doreen, were now hitting a brick wall, carrying their fight to an unseen bogey that refused to release their daughter and sister from its compulsive grip.

Finally in 2004, just before her fiftieth birthday, the attractive and intelligent girl from Ealing, London, surrendered to her fate. Her body refused to continue being subjected to the enormous abuse from which it was suffering. Lucia died and the rest of the family mourned. This young lady who had so many talents and natural gifts left this world childless and having never married.

Julie had lost a sister who could never be replaced. She'd lost her father and lived for a while, nursing her mother. She prayed that her sister and father would meet once again and perhaps heal the rift that was between them. The only comfort she had was the knowledge that Lucia and her father Patrick had both lived to witness Julie's success in

The Ballet.

'She was and continues to be a light in my life that will never be extinguished. She is now a part of the forest floor where the bluebells grow in the spring and where the light dances a ballet through the trees onto the now decaying ashes of those who are scattered there. Such a waste of beauty and talent'.

Julie Felix

About the Author

John F Plimmer was born and raised in the backstreets of Nechells, Birmingham. He retired from the West Midlands force following a 31 year illustrious career in which he was responsible for the investigation of more than 30 murder inquiries, all of which were detected successfully.

Following his retirement, he lectured in Law at Birmingham University and became a columnist and feature writer for The Sunday Mercury and Birmingham Evening Mail. Today, he frequently participates in discussions and interviews on police and legal subjects on both television and radio.

His television work has included working as a script consultant on popular programmes such as Dalziel and Pascoe, and Cracker.

His published works include a number of Home Office Blue Papers on Serious Crime Management and Covert Police Handling. He is the author of a number of published books which include In the Footsteps of the Whitechapel Murders (The Book Guild); Inside Track; Running with the Devil and The Whitechapel Murders (House of Stratus).

He is a dedicated reader of Louis L'Amour often giving L'Amour's work as the reason for spending years researching the old pioneering west.

His western novels include The Invisible Gun; Apache Justice and The Butte Conspiracy. His book, The Cutting Edge is a partially factual account of the biggest bank hoist ever committed in the history of the United Kingdom. The same work is the first of the popular series featuring Dan Mitchell, a British agent working for the Deep Cover Agency of the Foreign Office.

Other published books written by John Plimmer include:

Dan Mitchell Series:

Cutting Edge
Red Mist
The Food Mountain
The Neutron Claw
Chinese Extraction
Wrangel Island

Western Triology:

Tatanka Jake
Apache Justice
The Butte Conspiracy

Highwayman Series

In the Footsteps of the Highwaymen
The Wood Cutter
The Return
Treason

Also:

Inside Track
Running with the Devil
In the Footsteps of Capone
The World's most Notorious Serial Killers
In the Footsteps of the Whitechapel Murders
The Lost Paragons – The story of the West Midlands Serious
Crime Squad

Hilda's War
George's War
Brickbats & Tutus
Backstreet Urchins
The Circus Queen

The Victorian Detective's Casebook
A 15 book series

Printed in Great Britain
by Amazon

61541713R00187